FLIPPING HOUSES
AND
FINANCIAL FREEDOM INVESTING (UPDATED)

2-in-1 Book

Proven Methods to Find, Finance, Rehab, Manage and Resell Homes + Latest Reliable & Profitable Income Streams (Beginner's Guide)

REAL ESTATE INVESTING: FLIPPING HOUSES

Proven Methods to Find, Finance, Rehab, Manage and Resell Homes. Start to Generate Massive Passive Income Even with No Money Down

Flipping Houses

Table of Contents

Introduction 7

Chapter 1 – House-Flipping Fundamentals 12
   What Does 'Flipping Houses' Mean? 12
   Build a House-Flipping Mindset that Paves the Way for Success 15
   The 8 Steps to Flipping a House 19

Chapter 2 - Understanding the Market 26
   How to Properly Research & Analyze Your Local Real Estate Market . 26
   Following the 70% Rule 31
   Is it a Buyer's, Seller's, or Balanced Market? 35

Chapter 3 - No Money, No Problem 39
   Wholesaling: All You Need to Know to Get Started 39
   How to Get a Hard Money Loan 42
   Flipping Houses With No Money Using Private Investors 46

Chapter 4 - Choosing the Right Property 50
   Key Factors For Choosing The Right Location 50
   Features to Look For & Features to Avoid in Property 54
   Golden Rules for Picking Property 59
   How to Calculate Your Net Profit 63

Chapter 5 - It's All About Value 66
   The 4 Best Value-Boosting Renovations 66
   Curb Appeal: What It Is & How to Do It Right 72
   Small Updates for a Significantly More Desirable Home 74
   Green Improvements that Instantly Increase a Home's Value 77

Chapter 6 - Making It Shine 80
Putting Together the Rehab Dream Team 80
How to Find the Best Contractor for Your Property 85
Make It Shine While Minimizing Costs 89

Chapter 7 - Completing the Flip 93
The Lowdown on Selling Your Property Yourself vs. Through a Realtor 93
5 Best Marketing Strategies for Real Estate 96
How to Stage Your Property to Win Over Buyers 100

Chapter 8 - Staying Smart 104
House-Flipping Mistakes to Avoid at All Costs 104
4 Warning Signs Your House-Flip is Flopping 108
4 Exit Strategies to Always Keep in Mind 111

Conclusion – The Takeaways 116

Flipping Houses

Introduction

Has your cousin Jerry bragged about how he converted a $50K teardown into a $250K house? Do you have an eye for decaying properties on your commute to work and think to yourself "I could fix that up and sell that"? Do you fantasize about converting old abandoned shacks into livable, gorgeous homes until you become a real estate millionaire like Donald Trump? Maybe your hobby is to analyze real estate properties on the internet and you've accumulated knowledge about the real estate market in your area, enough that you're on the brink of getting into house flipping. House-flipping is the best way you to get your foot in real estate! It is the art of identifying future potential, investing in it and re-selling for a profit.

The average person looks at a house in bad shape and thinks: "That house is ugly". A house-flipper looks at a house in bad shape and thinks: "That house is my next paycheck!". A house-flipper is no different than an entrepreneur on Wall Street who invests in stocks: They identify a stock with future potential, invest their capital in it and cash out when the value increases. The difference is that house-flipping doesn't require luck and a house flippers can artificially raise the value of a property in as little as a few weeks with adequate repairs and renovations. This book will prepare you for the experience of a house-flipper by showing you the big secrets and the step-by-step to prepare you for your new life as a house flipper. The book will give you a kick in the butt and that last "push" you need if you're on the fence about house-flipping. It will give you all the details you need to reassure you and prepare you for your first flip.

We're here to hand it to you: The insider knowledge for all levels of investment - whether you're starting off broke or a millionaire, there are investments for every level obtainable. We'll explain which properties are investing in, so you don't waste your time on low-return properties with no potential. Just because the properties are cheap, doesn't mean they're going to give you returns. Don't worry, we'll tell you exactly where to look: Which states, the classification of neighborhoods, the types of properties that sell, the building permits, the zoning laws, the regulations, the contractors and finally how to sell your properties. We cover in great detail how to locate rare valuable properties, how to renovate, how to hire affordable contractors, cover legal fees and ultimately sell your property for the equivalent of a yearly salary.

1# Secret To House-Flipping

But before we start... Here's one secret you've never been told about house flipping:

- You don't have to be a millionaire!

That's right, you don't have to be a millionaire to get your foot in the door with house-flipping. You merely have to be a thousandnaire! We teach you numerous ways to acquire capital for your first property and how to present your investment as "low risk" to financiers who will bankroll your first flip. The key here is that there are investments for all income levels: If you have millions to spend, we'll teach you how to source-out high-value properties in class-A neighborhoods that you can flip for millions. If you have immediate access to capital, you can start flipping without consulting any financial institutions.

The US median home value is currently $230,000. That means that it's possible to find houses or condos for less than $230,000 and in many cases less than $100,000 that are still inhabitable. The mortgage on a $100,000 house can be as low as $400/month and the average down-payment is a mere 20%. Let's say you have no money to invest at all but you want to get into house-flipping. How easy would it be for you to accumulate $20,000 for a down-payment, fix up the house and flip it for a profit in 6 months? As you see, the barrier of entry is a lot lower than people imagine. If you have a 9-5 job and you save up for a year, there is a high chance you will be able to afford a down-payment. Once you've successfully flipped your first property, you can quit your job and get into house-flipping full-time – to become your own boss.

Pro Tip: The property you "flip" does not have to stand out, it just has to be livable. We encourage novices to start off by flipping average, working-class homes. Go for a drive in your city and observe the houses for 30 minutes. What do you notice? Average house. Average house. Average house. Over 90% of the real estate market is comprised up of average dwellings. Why focus on that one multi-million dollar home, when the middle-income market constitutes almost the entire market? Take a look at what constitutes the majority of your city. It's always going to be regular houses. This is where the money's at! Regular people need a place to live - your job is to provide them a home. Think: The retired veteran's property from across the street. Take your middle school's buddy house and flip that. A property doesn't have to be ran down to be flipped, it can be regular livable house which you upgrade by making small improvements.

The focus in this book is on dwellings for the average person will reside in and we make it our goal to identify multiple "flippable" properties until we start seeing consecutive ROI on our investments. If you focus on house-building and make it your #1 business, you are almost guaranteed to become a millionaire over the course of your lifetime. We focus on safe properties in high-growth areas that sell fast. You won't get rich in your first year, but you will immediately make enough money to pay the bills and finance much bigger deals. Moreover, if you flip one house that is a sign you can definitely flip another 10. Once you've flipped 10 houses, you can flip an entire neighborhood. Once you flipped a neighborhood, you can move on to buildings and commercial properties. Once you get into buildings and commercial properties, the sky is the limit! We explain the safest, idiot-proof house-flipping methods that beginners with little/no investment capital can use to capitalize on the housing market.

#2 Secret To House-Flipping

Here's the second secret about house-flipping:

- You don't have to know "trades" to fix houses!

If you think you need to know about plumbing, painting, wiring and roofing to flip a house, you couldn't be more wrong. Your job as a house-flipper is to do the administrative tasks: To identify properties with high potential, to convince financiers to put up the initial money, to hire contractors who fix the property and ultimately flip the house. You don't need to know the first thing about roof shingles and/or Persian rugs, you hire people to do that for you. In essence, you must be the person who "brings it all together". You're the missing link between all those contractors, bankers and buyers. Your job is to ensure everyone sees a return on their investment, which ultimately provides you with a return on your investment. Your job is to persuade the investors, to sign off the checks for the blue-collar workers and provide buyers with an adequate livable space in which they can reside. This book will prepare you for each step of the way.

#3 Secret To House-Flipping

Here's the third secret about house-flipping:

- The market itself will increase the value of your property!

On average, the yearly median home value in the US increases by 3-6%. Example: If you purchased a house for $300,000 in 3 years it would be worth between $330,000 and $360,000. That is $30,000-60,000 increase in value while doing absolutely nothing! If you sat on it for a decade that same property would be worth at least $400,000. That's $100,000 in the bank, and don't forget you still own the place. House-flippers obsess over "fixing up" the house in order to solidify its value. Bear in mind livable houses will always increase in value as the economy goes up - one can sit and down nothing and the value of the property will increase in as little as a few years.

How many people do you know who bought a property for $50,000 in 1980 and that same property is now worth $1,5M? The increase in value is through the roof. The only question that remains: How do you predict which areas are going to gentrify over the next 5-10 years? How do you analyze the type of neighborhoods that are worth investing in and will remain wealthy? In this book we focus on areas that sell immediately and help you identify the hottest markets in the US. This way your first property will not remain on the market for longer than a week - you'll have people calling you and begging to give you their money.

#4 Secret To House Flipping

The fourth and final secret to house-flipping:

- ***You can flip your first house in 3 months!***

House-flipping is not an infinite process where you wait for a year before you can sell a house. You can flip a house in as little as 12 weeks! All you have to do is purchase is investigate the market, purchase a property, fix it up and sell it. We explain how to do each step in great detail in the book. Many of you will have different levels of knowledge about house-flipping. If you have no idea what it stands for, pay extra attention in the first chapters. The speed and efficiency will depend on your capital: If you have capital to invest immediately, you can flip a house in as little as a four weeks. This is because you can finance the house and repairs immediately, while someone without immediate access to capital will have to wait for approval and plan out their investments months in advance. In both cases the same principles and methods listed in this book apply!

How To Navigate This Book

We lay out the basics for beginners: If you don't know where to start, the terminology, what mindset you need to obtain to be successful in house-flipping, how to finance your first house and the neighborhoods to invest in, focus on the introductory chapters. If you have a more advanced level of knowledge and you wish to learn more about how to lower your costs for contractors and which houses sell in the current market and how to finance bigger deals – move straight to the advanced chapters.

Chapter 1 – House-Flipping Fundamentals

What Does 'Flipping Houses' Mean?

You're about to become a house-flipper - congratulations! You're about to experience the glamour of the "Sold!" sign on your first house flip, and you are a few months away from handing the keys of your first flip to your first client. You are in for a journey: You're about to see your investments materialize and a big, fat check to compensate you for all your hard work. The key to real-estate riches and making the right moves is to be diligent about details. That has everything to do with your property purchases, the expenses you accumulate and putting your home on the market. We'll teach you step-by-step how to minimize your initial expenses on your first purchase, how to minimize your expenses on the upgrades and finally make the average US salary on every single flip. This is our end goal for everyone reading this!

House-Flipping: The Definition

Important: House-flipping is not about taking houses and turning them upside down! It's about buying a house as an investment, improving it and selling it for a profit. "House Flipping" is sometimes referred to as "wholesale real estate investing" and it's a real-estate investment strategy in which you purchase a property with the intention of re-selling it instead of settling down in it yourself.

You've seen many successful, well-dressed real-estate millionaires flipping houses on TV and sharing their experience with the world. You want to emulate them and become a success story, or maybe you want to flip a house to add to your existing income. Three are more than 200,000 houses being bought, fixed and re-sold in the United

States each year. If you could only fix up 10 house a year, you would be a millionaire in as little as a few years. Does this sound incentivizing? There are people in the US currently flipping 5 new houses a week and remodeling them. The hardest "flip" is usually your very first flip: You don't know what to expect, how much contractors will charge you, you don't know how permits work and you don't know how to buy/sell a property. Worry not, this guide has the nitty-gritty details you need to give you the confidence for each step. Pay close attention as this might change your life.

How House Flipping Works

To be successful in house flipping, there are usually two ways in which investors use to make a profit: 1) From appreciation in a "hot" real estate market or 2) Capital investments in a property which increase its value. Most house-flippers choose the latter and purchase an average property and equip it with state-of-the-art amenities such as a new floor, paint, kitchen, and bathroom. If a property costs $100,000 and the upgrades cost $40,000, the investor can easily sell that home for $200,000. The "strategy" for flipping is identical to other investment principles: buying low and selling high. Time is of the essence in house-flipping the costs increase the longer a flipper has to pay for insurance and property taxes rise, hence the average "flip" takes 6 months. Established flippers might purchase 5-10 new properties each week.

But stop! Before we reveal the insider secrets of house flipping, before we teach you the mindsets that are conducive to a successful flip, and before we tell you how to purchase properties for below market-value - we must teach you the very basics of house-flipping and what they entail.

House-Flipping Basics: ARV ("After Repair Value")

Pro Tip: The most important term in house-flipping is "ARV" - "After Repair Value". If you plan to sell a home for $250,000, your RAV for that home is $250,000. Once the home is remodeled, spanking-shiny and ready to be listed on the market – this is the ARV (the final selling price on the market). Remember the term ARV as it refers to the final value of the home once repairs are carried out. The ARV formula is simple to understand: Original home value + Repair costs = ARV (after repair value).

House-flipping revolves around ARV as all calculations stem from the final investment value which the investor plans to invest into the property. Remember what the acronym ARV stands for as you'll be hearing that very often in this book, and among your house-flipping crowd. ARV determines the repairs and upgrades you'll have to make to a property before you're prepared to list it on the market. What are the rules of ARV and how to calculate expenses?

House-Flipping Basics: The 70% Rule Of ARV

The 70% rule is the most famous rule-of-thumb in house-flipping. This rule helps to calculate the expenses on a home before you even put down a payment on a property. The 70% rule commands that a house-flipper should not pay more than 70% of the total ARV (after repair value) minus the repair costs involved. This gives leeway for a house-flipper to make at least 30% profit on each sale. In some cases the profit can be as much as 40%, however, as a rule of thumb - investors stick to a safe 30%. Remember that ARV is not just the initial costs and the repairs, but it's the final value of the property.

The 70% Rule:

→ **(ARV x 0.70) – Repair Costs = X (maximum amount you should spend on a property).**

Pro Tip: Take your calculator and calculate the first house-flip you'll make. For the examples below, we'll take two houses - one with a value of $200,000 that requires $40,000 in repairs and another with a value of $150,000 that requires $30,000 in repairs.

Example #1: $200,000 x 0.70 - $40,000 = $100,000.

Example #2: $150,000 x 0.70 - $30,000 = $75,000

In total, the investor should NOT exceed spending of $100,000 for the acquisition of the first property in order to close a $200,000 sale at the end. For the second house, the investor should NOT spend more than $75,000 on a house in order to sell it for $150,000.

The 70% rule is important because each house is different and requires a different set of repairs. Some houses might be worth $200,000 and require only $20,000 in repairs while other houses of the same value would require $50,000 in repairs. The ARV is the most important calculation you'll have to make in house-flipping in order to determine your profitability at the end. The 70% rule provides a "buffer" in case of unexpected expenses on your first flip which would increase the cost of repairs and prevent you from making a profit.

Ran your first calculation? Congrats, you're 50% of the way to becoming a house-flipper! Now that you know how to calculate your expenses in advance, we'll get into the success mindset you need to obtain and cover each step of the investment process in detail.

Build a House-Flipping Mindset that Paves the Way for Success

House-flipping requires mental shifts that are conducive to being effective in the business in general. A house-flipper can't think like an average person – a house-flipper must think 6 months in advance and have the know-how to calibrate to construction problems once they arise. The challenge of house-flipping is to prepare for the finish line before you even start and learn how to deal with problems as they arise, without losing sight of the big picture. The key principles of house-flipping are the following 5 principles: 1) Preparation, 2) efficiency, 3) decisiveness, 4) action-taking and 5) patience. The way those principles apply to the day-to-day of house flipping are in the mindsets which you will learn below. These principles and mind-shifts are conductive to a house-flipper who wishes to execute their flip in the most efficient way possible:

Top 5 Principles Of House-Flipping

Flipping Houses

1) Preparation

The average house-flip takes 6 months from purchase to sale. On average, you'll have to spend a month researching a property, gathering documents, hiring lawyers, preparing the finances and signing off the checks. This process can be lengthy, especially on wholesale purchases such as foreclosed properties. Once you've purchased the property, you'll have to hire individual contractors for each step of the way. If the rooms need painting, you'll have to source out painting contractors. If you need the wires changed, you'll have to source out electricians. All of them bid their unique price and you must estimate the cost of each repair before you purchase the property. Once you're fully prepared, you can make the purchase and start fixing the property until it's done. Preparation work is the most crucial process for ensuring you make a profit at the end.

2) Efficiency

The way you execute each process will determine the final sale price of the property. Did you hire poor contractors who messed up the tiles on the floor? This can take away from the impression clients have on the property and lower your sale price. As a property developer, you must care for each detail and apply diligence to make sure the small repairs you make will match the big picture of the home.

Example: It's safer to paint each room in a single white color than paint each room individually. In areas that are out of your control such as hiring contractors - you must be efficient in choosing the best contractors possible.

3) Decisiveness

House-flipping is not like on TV! The real day-to-day of house-flipping is messy. Many times you will run into problems you never expected which can increase the costs of your repairs.

Example: You might discover molding on the roof that requires you to change the entire roof. You might be faced with a roach infestation in the bathroom. Despite the fact that you carried out a thorough investigation upon purchase, you will still experience hurdles along the way. Prepare for this by being decisive! Don't dwell on complex solutions but focus on the simplest solution you can find. In most cases the solutions to big problems are simple. If the roof needs replacing, allocate a higher percentage of your budget on the roof - this is more essential than picking out fancy tiles for the bathroom. Make the call!

4) Action-Taking

Remember: Action cures fear! Action-taking will remove the paranoia you have about things going wrong or your investment going down the drain. Once you're actually in the thick of your repairs, you will start enjoying them and you'll find house-flipping fun. You're creating value for society on many levels: You're providing liquidity for people who you bought the house from in the first place. You're giving jobs to contractors who feed their families on your repairs. You're doing a service to the future owners of the property by providing them a home. Remind yourself of that every time you doubt yourself and go to work!

5) Patience

Most houses are flipped within 6-12 months. Want to do it in 1 month? It's possible but you will likely have to work around the clock and have connections with contractors who can help you immediately. Most quality contractors are booked months in advance and you will have to be patient in terms of legal permits which can take weeks or months depending on the state/municipality. Patience is crucial when you the property is fixed too - it might sit on the market for longer than you expect unless it's in a "hot" market. Be patient because this is not something you'll accomplish overnight. Prepare for at least half a year on your first flip. Once you've done that, try to cut the time on your next flip by half. Build up efficiency gradually.

Top 3 Mind-Shifts For House Flipping

The principles of house-flipping apply to all areas of success - there are also specific mind-shifts which apply only to house-flipping. Use the mind-shifts below to ensure you end up successful in your house-flipping endeavors:

Mind-shift #1: Focus On Speed

Limit the amount of time you take to complete all transactions: Buying, fixing and selling. The key mind-shift you must make it to focus on speed in the short-term and have patience in the long-term. How do you align the two? You must have faith that no matter how long the flip takes, you will be able to pull it off. However, you must accelerate your day-to-day in order to speed up the process of gathering finances, hiring contractors, legalizing the building and selling the fixed property. Your sole focus on your day-to-day should be on speed instead of maximizing profit. Each day your property sits on the market will end up costing you more and this is why accelerating the process is crucial. If you can flip the whole property within 1 month, do it! There is no "rule" saying the property has to sit on the market for 6 months. Always cut down the time in half: If you think a flip is going to take a year, try to do it in 6 months!

REMEMBER: The longer you hold on to a property, the more you're risking your finances. Many things can go wrong with the property if you hold it for months: It could be burglarized, destroyed in a hurricane, the quality of repairs deteriorates, etc. There are also added costs which you must account for before purchase: The utilities, mortgage payment, insurance payments, property taxes, and more. Example of hidden-costs: Insurance for house-flips will cost 2x regular home insurance because you must purchase "vacancy insurance" for the home.

Mind-shift #2: Cheap Is Not Always Profitable

Don't rush to buy a house! There are many reasons why a property is cheap: It can be a sketchy neighborhood, no access to infrastructure, or back taxes owed on the property. Do you remember headlines of houses going for $10 or even $1 in Detroit? Those same houses can have $10,000 or even $20,000 in back-taxes owed by the previous owners that weren't paid for decades. The new owner will have to pay those taxes out of pocket. If the neighborhood doesn't have access to good schools, families will be reluctant to purchase your property. We explain how to shift neighborhood classifications and identify thriving neighborhoods where you can purchase properties on the cheap.

Mind-shift #3: Overestimate Your Initial Costs

Things can always go wrong in house-flipping. Do you think because you bought in a rich area that your property is safe? You could purchase a home in a safe, wealthy, educated district and the contractors could ruin everything. Many times flippers end up barely making their money back or even losing money on their first flip. This is due to overhead on expenses they didn't prepare for in advance.

Example: Let's say you can paint. You need to paint 3 rooms in the house and you think it would take you 5 hours to paint each room. If you seek out contractors who work for $30/h, that would mean they would charge you $150 per room. However, many of them will bid $300-500 per room. Why does that happen? You might over-estimate how fast you can paint each room yourself. The contractors might need more time, or they have overhead, or maybe they're even plain greedy! Always expect to spend more than you initially calculate or consult multiple contractors for a bid until you can decisively conclude the average cost of each repair.

Once you've internalized the aforementioned principles and mind-shifts, you're ready for the war of house-flipping! Bring it on!

The 8 Steps to Flipping a House

It's time to pull up your sleeves and do the dirty work! Excited? Let's get the ball rolling. House-flipping is not like in the TV shows. You don't magically purchase a house, renovate it in the snap of a finger and $50,000 magically appears in your bank account. You must do due-diligence research of neighborhoods, finance the purchase, follow zoning laws, carry out renovations and ultimately sell the property.

Flipping Houses

Pro Tip: House-flipping is "messy" in real life. You will never sell a property the way you imagined to, and each property will require individual attention and care. One property might work smooth and fast, and another property might become a nightmare to renovate. The guidelines below are only to give you an idea as to what to expect. Moreover, there is no "ultimate" way to house-flip. You must find your ideal method yourself! Let's say you refuse to hire realtors and sell the property yourself (to keep their 5% commission). There is no written law that you must use a realtor! You might also refuse to hire contractors and bring a family member to do the renovations yourself. It's up to you to discover what works for you.

The top 6 steps to house-flipping will help get you get your foot in the world of house-flipping. The steps we present will help you become a professional on your first flip - avoiding the mistakes that novices make. For example, many novices rush to purchase their first property and don't carry out inspections which end up costing them more than their profit. If you follow our steps, you will know which houses to buy and use an inspector who will verify the house is in good shape for renovations. We also teach you which renovations to carry out and which ones to skip. Advance stages such as the capital gains tax and zoning laws will be explained further, but if you follow the 6-steps you will be successful on your first flip:

1) Network With Real Estate Experts

New to house-flipping? Forget about the house! Forget about banks and renovations. Start by talking to actual house-flippers in your area. Visit an event for real estate and network with people who flip houses for a living. This will be crucial as they have connections to all the contractors you'll need: electricians, roofers, plumbers, general contractors, painters, HVAC people, handymen, etc. You will eventually need the assistance of some of those people. In general, one could look up "x area + contractor" to find a local contractor, but if you know house-flippers who have used those contractors before it will make your job a lot easier.

Flipping Houses

Warning: Many times a contractor will promise you "We'll get it done in 1 week" and a month later they're still playing with the drywall. You need to get in touch with verified contractors who carry out work efficiently. The best way to do this is to consult people who are like you, before you even attempt your first flip. In most cases those people will also have "insider" information as to bureaucracy and flipping secrets that you would only discover after years in the business.

How do you source out real estate people? Won't they see you as competition? We hear you, but the answer is simple - pay them. If you contact a flipper or an established real estate firm (both of which work in construction and hire the same contractors), you can offer to pay them $1000 to have them "on call" once you run into problems and need access to information about contractors. This is a small price to pay for access to the best contractors in your area. You're making them an "offer they can't refuse" because they know they have to do minimal work and it's more likely to work than demanding their connections empty-handed.

2) Research Neighborhoods

In real estate there are "classes" based on the gentrification level of a neighborhood. There are only 4 classes: A, B, C and D. A-class neighborhoods are the "elite" neighborhoods in a city. Class-A's are populated by the most affluent individuals, celebrities, politicians, and the general upper echelon of society. The expense of a house in a Class-A neighborhood will depend on the city. In more affluent cities, the average going price for a home could be $1M. In less wealthier cities, a Class-A neighborhoods might have an average price of $500,000.

Class-A flips are the safest as the houses are always in demand and they have the best access to infrastructure, schools and safety. Class-B neighborhoods are "upper middle income" neighborhoods: The most typical representation of the "American Dream". Class-B houses can be quite sizable. Class-C neighborhoods are considered "working class" neighborhoods, and are usually populated by middle-income residents. Class-D neighborhoods are low-income neighborhoods and properties there cost less.

What are the best neighborhoods? It depends - the cheapest class-D neighborhoods might have many "great deals" but insurance premiums are higher as the risk of crime and home invasions increases. Class-A neighborhoods are mostly out of reach for novice flippers. Most novice flippers start with Class-C or Class-B neighborhoods.

Pro Tip: Your flip is not confined to neighborhood research. You could technically purchase a rural, isolated property and flip that property. Neighborhood classification is merely an economic indicator for the prosperity of a neighborhood.

3) Calculate Total Budget

It's time to bust out your calculator! Calculate your budget, how much you can afford on the property and how much will go on renovations. This is not hard - it's common sense! Let's say you only have $20,000 to set aside for repairs, in that case you should stay away from $500,000 houses. The ideal flip for you would be a house in the sub $100,000< range. If you have $200,000 to spare on renovations, you should consider getting into class-A houses estimated at $500,000-1M. As a rule of thumb, estimate that the down-payment on the house will be 20%. In this case, there are clear differences between a down-payment on a $500,000 house and down-payment on a $50,000 house. Calculate how much you can spend on the house pre-renovations.

Once you've calculated the down-payment and total cost of acquisition, you must factor in the renovation expenses. The sale price should never exceed the price of acquisition, renovation and maintenance (utilities, property taxes, insurance, etc). Let's say you add a $15,000 kitchen, $10,000 bathroom, $5000 in yearly maintenance costs and other carrying costs - add the highest expenses you expect and combine that with the acquisition cost. Now add an unexpected structural problem to stay safe. Don't forget that even after you sell, the average gross profit on a flip in the United States is

$60,000. Once capital gains taxes set in, it's even less. The lower your renovation costs, the more money in your pocket at the end of the flip!

4) Finance The Purchase

It's time to take out the liquid for the purchase - you must prepare money before you start visiting houses, talking to real-estate owners or realtors. If you have access to capital you can skip this part entirely and focus on the acquisition! However, if you don't you must secure the funds yourself. The good news: You don't have access to 6-figure sums, there are many workarounds that will supply you the capital you need. Most people either opt for bank lending or they rely on private lending. We cover how to secure a bank loan or consult private lenders who will finance the whole purchase for a cut at the final flip price.

Once you've secured funding, that's when the fun starts. Keep in mind you're paying interest from day 1. The bank interest on borrowed money for a property is tax-deductible, and despite cuts in the Jobs Act, the interest is not a 100% cut. Once you add in the principal, capital gains taxes and double rates for vacancy insurance, none of those are deductible.

This is the right time to consult an accountant or a lawyer - those professionals will estimate the total cost for all legal/tax expenses and allow you to estimate the cost on the flip, renovations and hidden-charges. This will reassure you that the purchase you're making is a safe one.

5) Investigate The Property

Secured the money? Ready to get the keys? Wait, don't rush to buy that house yet! New house-flippers rush this and a month later they discover a structural problem that eats up their entire renovation budget. Send them a home inspector first. A home inspector is a professional who can be sent on-location to investigate the entire property for any kind of structural problem. They will give you a detailed report as to the state of the property, the renovations necessary and the total expenses for all the repairs needed.

Flipping Houses

Home inspectors are imperative to ensuring the property you're about to purchase is structural sound and that the internal infrastructural and mechanical systems are functional. Once the inspector verifies you won't run into "unpleasant surprises", you can start signing checks and shaking hands.

6) Acquire The Property

The exciting stuff! Once you've investigated a property, it's time to get the keys to the house. This property will now belong to you and it becomes your responsibility. There are many ways to purchase a property. Most flippers purchase directly from sellers to avoid agent fees. To find the best "deals" you might purchase foreclosed properties where the owner failed to make a payment or a tragic accident happened such as death, divorce or financial distress. It's not "immoral" to purchase from these people, as you're providing liquidity that will help them start a new life. No matter how you purchase the property, you will have to sign off legal papers and get the procedure notarized. Consider hiring a lawyer for the process, to verify there are no "loopholes" and that you actually own the property. If something looks fishy, refuse to sign. Let your lawyer have a detailed look at every paper and then put your signature on it.

IMPORTANT: You must prepare for inspections that the municipality will send out after you buy a property. The local municipality will send inspectors who will consult with you and "investigate" your property to ensure it follows municipal building codes. Inspections will be rigid in most "prime" neighborhoods that maintain high standards. Virtually all municipalities will send inspections before you're allowed to sell a property. If the investigators detect something is wrong with the property you will have to spend more time and money fixing it until it meets their standards.

7) Renovate The Property

You have the keys to the house – what now? You must renovate it to increase its value. This is where the "sweat equity" kicks in, the stuff they don't show on TV. This is also when ugly surprises come up.

Flipping Houses

What if you find out the bathroom is infested with roaches at night? You could never guess that even with an inspector. You will have to hire contactors to exterminate the infestation - the same with rats, ants or any rodents on the property. Is the paint bad in one room? You'll have to paint every room to make sure that doesn't stand out. You must calibrate to the needs of each individual property. This is when you'll need assistance from your real-estate friends who can put you in touch with contractors: electricians, plumbers, carpenters, roofers, gardeners, etc. Even if you execute everything perfectly there is no guarantee your contractors won't mess up! If they tell you they'll get it done in 2 days, they might discover the job is harder and requires a week of repairs. Expect delays and increased charges.

Pro Tip: To make more money you must spend less on renovations. How do you pull that off? Learn to "fix" things yourself. If you're handy with a hammer, if you can install a kitchen sink, if you know how to roof or hang drywall - you have skills that will save you thousands of dollars off the bat. If you can't work with equipment, lack the skills or outright don't want to get your hands dirty - there are always professionals who will deploy to your location and get the job done.

8) Sell The Property

This is the final part - the part where you see 5 or 6 digit amounts hit your bank account! There are ways to save money on the sale too! If you don't know any trades but you like selling, you can sell your own property directly. There are many ways to sell a property online which we'll explain further. If you turn to a real-estate agency they will offer to sell your property for 5% commission and the lowest they'll go is 4%. This is a hefty sum to pay on your first property. Why give it away when you can sell the property yourself? We'll explain how to tap into the "for sale by owner" market and sell your property within a matter of weeks.

Chapter 2 - Understanding the Market

How to Properly Research & Analyze Your Local Real Estate Market

You stumbled upon a great deal in suburban New Jersey: A $90,000 house with access to schools, hospitals and good infrastructure. How do you analyze if the $90,000 price is adequate for that location, square footage and structural shape? Analyzing the immediate area of your property will help you determine the average price of a house. Don't make the call yet: It's time to search for previous "Sold" properties in the area that will give you comparable properties to know if you're getting a good deal or being ripped off! Those properties are called "comps" in the real estate industry - identical properties with identical square footage (that sold in your area recently). Comps are only viable if they sold in the last 6 months. If a property sold a year ago, it doesn't tell you much about the current state of the market. This is why accumulating recent data is essential for comps, and then cross-referencing the data with an appraiser who can estimate the home value based on the maintenance level and structural integrity.

To discover comps for your property, you must analyze properties within a 1/2 mile range of your property that sold within the last 3-6 months. Each property you stumble upon that sold can be classified as a "comp". However, you must seek out properties with similar or identical square footage to determine the average price. There are tools that can help you narrow down your research such as Zillow and Redfin that provide "estimates" as to the average house value in each zip code and can vaguely estimate the price of a house using mapping data. However, to get accurate real-world data you have to analyze properties that were actually sold as estimates can be completely off-base.

What happens if it's impossible to discover properties that sold of similar square footage? To get around a shortage of "sold" properties, you must analyze other properties that are larger or smaller that can give you a value comparison, and estimate by doing the math on the difference.

Example: You have your $90,000 property in NJ and the property is 2000 sq ft. If you discover a larger property such as one of 2500 sq ft. that sold in the area for the same price, you might be getting a bad deal. However, if you find similar prices for sold properties then this is potentially a good deal. At the end, it's important to cross-reference your comps with a local realtor and/or appraiser who can estimate the value of a property and indicators that might increase or decrease property value such as proximity to amenities, healthcare/educational institutions and general shape of the property. Realtors deal with local real estate markets, making them more effective at determining local home value.

Pro Tip: Realtors can help you estimate the sale price on your house flip in advance. Once you've gathered a list of comps, you will have access to data for the average listing price for a home of that square footage in your area. You can then consult a realtor to help you with the final calculations. The realtor will help you identify the most accurate comps, analyze the property you're trying to acquire and calculate the final potential price for based on the condition of the property.

4 Steps Of Using Comps To Determine Home Value

Once you've found a suitable property, it's time to gather your list of "comps"! Not all properties that sold in your area are eligible. The "comps" are only homes that sold in recent time (3-6 months) and have similar features to your home. Before you put down a payment on a house, you must analyze comps and identify which one is the closest to your future property. You must either use online tools that enable you to research properties in your area using maps, or Google "Neighborhood + sold properties" to discover realtors who sold properties in your area and find out if they sold a property of similar square footage. The following 4 steps will help you identify comps for your future property:

Flipping Houses

Step #1) Identify Properties In 1/2 Mile Radius

Location, location, location! The properties have to be in the same neighborhood or within a short 1/2 mile radius to qualify as comps. Home value can increase and decrease within a single mile because certain areas are blocked off from major roads or have terrain difficulties that cut them off from receiving infrastructure that reflect in the listing price. Find a list of all the closest properties that sold recently and calculate the average value based on the information. Don't look at listings for sale, but focus on properties that sold already. This will give you an accurate estimate as to the average price per square foot. If a comp is too far from your property, it might give you the wrong idea as to the value which could be higher or lower.

Step #2) Identify Similar Interior Features

The home you're comparing to must have similar quality features and interior. If a home has a very modern interior, elevators, high-tech kitchen, and other amenities - this can increase the value of the property exponentially. This is why you shouldn't compare "fixed" properties to a ran down property. A qualified comp should have identical interior features to the property you're considering purchasing. If you buy a semi-ran-down property, find semi-ran-down comps in similar shape. If you buy a well-maintained property, find other well-maintained properties. The closer a property is to your purchase, the higher the accuracy of the value appraisal.

Step #3) Identify Similar Square Footages

The home must be of similar or identical square footage to be considered a comp. If you're buying a 2000 sq ft. home you won't get a lot of insight comparing that to a 5000 sq. ft. home. Try to narrow down comps based on the size of the home and follow that up by removing the difference. Let's say a 2000 sq. ft home goes for $100,000 in an area. If you see 4000 sq ft. homes going for $200,000-250,000 in that same area, you can easily determine the average home value. Square footage is usually the biggest value-indicator.

4) Identify Similar Constructions

Construction type can affect the house price as many construction methods have changed over the years. This is particularly true in states such as Florida where after Hurricane-regulations, many new homes are now Hurricane-proof and command higher real-estate prices than old homes. The structure also reflects in the home insurance prices as outdated homes will command much higher insurance or be refused by the insurers outright. Analyze when the comps were built and the structural difference between your property and the way those differences reflect in the final price.

Real Estate Websites For Comps

Which tools are the best for gathering data? Analyze local properties by looking at the biggest real estate websites that can give you a list of "Sold" properties, home value estimates for each neighborhood and current listings. The following websites are the most reliable tools for the house-flipper:

Zillow

Zillow is currently the largest real-estate website in the United States. Zillow exclusively specializes in the US real-estate market and can give you detailed value estimates for every house in the US. The company operates on a map-based principle and once you've narrowed in on a location, it can estimate the value of each house by the average listing price and sold price in the area + indicators such as square footage taken by government data. The company makes researching properties in your area a breeze, and it can narrow them down by price + give you access to public records and recently sold properties in every area. Zillow is actually getting into house-flipping themselves and their agents are tasked to sell each property in less than 3 months: It's the go-to website for a house-flipper because their database is the largest.

Trulia

Trulia is an excellent tool for house-flippers because it provides insight that might affect the home value such as "local insights". These insights can make you aware of things you didn't realize on-location while you were looking at a property: Crime reports, school ratings, local community events, and the website even has discussion boards. A home-flipper can have a big-picture perspective on their acquisition by using Trulia's detailed analysis of each property.

Redfin

Redfin is a popular real estate tool: It's main standout feature is the 3D walk-through feature that enables you to look at properties "inside the home" by walking around as if you were on location. They have relatively low listing fees too. However, this tool does not have the extensive analysis features of Zillow and Trulia.

Realtor.com

Realtor.com used to be the biggest real estate listing site and it currently holds its own by providing one of the most accurate value appraisal tools that can identify current home value for each home in the US. The site also has tracking tools for real estate investors that can track your profits.

Hiring An Appraiser

Once you've gathered your comps, analyzed properties using online tools, consulted with realtors - the final step you should take is to hire a professional appraiser who can walk in the property and analyze everything for a final estimate. They can give you a non-biased perspective as to the real value of the home. If your comps and research come close to that of the appraiser, you can be certain you're getting a great price!

Pro Tip: Appraisers provide different value-insight than realtors or online tools. They analyze the home by stepping inside and testing all the individual features. They will analyze the property location, structural layout/convenience, required improvements for the bathrooms/kitchen, HVAC conditions which might require repairs, and the condition of the interior/exterior. Once they've had all these things in account and ran their calculations, they will give you a final estimate. The appraiser puts the final piece of the puzzle together as they can summarize their calculation and you can compare that to the data you've gathered online. To find an appraiser, either consult with realtor for a referral or Google local appraisers.

Step On The The Property

There is nothing that can indicate whether your property will sell or not than actually setting foot on the property: You'll instantly know if it "feels right" or if the property feels like a bad deal the second you step on the property yourself! Ask yourself: Would you live on this property? Put yourself in the shoes of a customer and decide if you would live in that property and which upgrades you'd want for yourself. Do you feel safe in the area? Do you like the shape of the house? What bothers you about the interior? If you make the property livable for yourself, there is a high chance someone else will find it livable as well.

Following the 70% Rule

You must choose between 2 properties: The first costs $100,000 and has a bad interior and the second costs $115,000 but has a decent interior? Which one should you buy and flip? How do you estimate how much you should pay for a property once you've narrowed down the neighborhood research and know the average going value per square foot? The answer is the 70% rule! The 70% rule is the rule-of-thumb for house-flippers because it leave 30% profit at the end of each flip that you can use to cover your lending fees and other small/unplanned costs. A house-flipper is not "safe" because they're always prone to unexpected charges and the 70% rule ensures your investment is safe from structural failures, delayed repair charges, takeover fees and more. Novices make the mistake of buying a house without accounting for the 70% rule, and then they either make no profit or they even lose money. This is why smart house-flippers calculate all their final profits and expenses before they even purchase a house.

Flipping Houses

How Does The 70% Rule Work?

To avoid over-bidding or loss of profits, the 70% rule can help you determine the maximum you should spend on each property. If a house is going to be worth $100,000 at the end, you probably shouldn't be bidding even half of that amount at the start. The 70% rule is applied before flippers put down a bid on a property. Flippers must do their calculations 3 months in advance in order to determine the ARV (final sale price) and take away 70% of that which is the maximum they should spend on an unfixed property. There is a simple formula which a flipper can use to run the basic calculations.

Pro Tip: Remember that what you pay at the start is the biggest indicator as to how much profit you'll be left with post-flip. If you overpay for the property, you will make less profits for yourself and your investors. However, if you bid below the 70% max-value and you negotiate a property for less than that amount, you're likely to be left with huge profits at the end of the flip. Therefore, your job is to estimate what 70% ARV is for a particular property, take that away and negotiate the house for that amount and/or less.

What Is The 70% Formula?

The 70% rule is a formula to determine the maximum price you should be paying for a house pre-flip. The 70% rule applies for properties on all levels: abandoned homes, normal homes in working-class areas and even high-value homes in class-A neighborhoods. The 70% in essence dictates that an investor should not pay more than 70% of the final value post-renovations. This leaves investors with a 30% surplus that comprises their final profit and other miscellaneous costs that might arise. The 70% rule functions on the principle of ARVL: After repair value. Once you've added-up the total renovation costs on top of the original home value - you have your ARV. You then subtract 70% from that ARV and you have the maximum figure you should pay for the property. If we apply simple math, and the ARV of a house is $100,000 and it needs $30,000 in repairs, this means that the investor should not pay more than $40,000 for that property. We'll take a detailed look at the math below.

The 70% rule is a general rule, however, it's not written in stone. You can technically flip a house at no-profit to show yourself that flipping houses is possible. You could try to invent your own 60% rule and only bid at 60% of the ARV, which many people will likely take too (if they're in desperate need of liquid).

The Golden 70% Rule Formula

The formula of the 70% rule is the following:

ARV x 70% - Renovation Costs = Max Bid Price

Alternative formula: ARV x 0.70 - Renovation Costs = Max Bid Price

Real estate investing carries hidden costs that are not outright visible such as the initial financing/lender costs, settlement costs, realtor/listing costs, carrying costs and other soft costs such as property taxes, insurance and capital gains taxes. Once you add in unforeseen renovation costs, you must set aside at least 30% in profits to account for all those costs at once. This way you're not caught by surprise when your contractor overbids by $2000 and you can't find a smaller bid but you planned to only spend $500.

Calculations Using The 70% Rule

For the purpose of averages, we'll take the average home value of a United States home: $230,000. How much should you pay for a $230,000 house (if the home is worth $230,000 after renovations)? Let's account for all costs associated with buying a $230K home.

ARV (After-Repair-Value): $230,000.

Renovation Costs: $50,000 (example: $20,000 for a kitchen, $15,000 for a bathroom, and $15,000 for paint, interior upgrades, lawn upgrades, etc).

Flipping Houses

Renovation Reserve Budget: $10,000 (take away 20% of your total renovation budget as a buffer for unexpected expenses and contractor surcharges - you might not always spend this, but to stay safe!).

Settlement Costs: $10,000.

Finance Costs (Interest Rates): $5000.

Total Costs: $75,000.

The total amount of how much you'll have to set aside to flip the average US home of $230,000 is $75,000 for repair costs. In many cases this can become $65,000 or less if you hire the right contractors, sell the property yourself, spend less on renovations, negotiate better lending rates, etc. The 70% rule is not written in stone, but for the purpose of averages we'll take the estimate of $75,000.

Now let's apply the golden formula:

$230,000 x 0.70 - $75,000 = $86,000

Conclusion: According to the 70% rule, a flipper who wants to flip a home worth $230,000 at the end should not bid more than $86,000 - however, that's not how it works in practice because it doesn't account for your estimated profit. Let's say you wish to make a $40,000 profit at the end of this sale. If you started with a $230,000 ARV estimate and you took away your $75,000 expenses and then you took away your estimated profits of $40,000, you would reach a maximum bid price of $115,000. You could make the $40,000 profit by offering anything less than $115,000, but it's possible to make more if you bid lower and spend less on renovations and miscellaneous costs. The final profit will be based on the extensiveness of your renovations, your experience negotiating and flipping, the risk level and the time the deal takes.

Warning: Do not over-estimate the ARV. The 70% Rule only helps you identify instant costs, but it will never reflect the actual repair costs once you're on the ground because each property requires unique treatment. Always be cautious and conservative with your ARV estimates and use worst-case-scenario numbers for your renovation costs. You won't be able to get inside a property and estimate repairs if you're buying a foreclosed home, and this is something to consider when you're on the hunt for good deals. You'll have to run those calculations in advance.

Is it a Buyer's, Seller's, or Balanced Market?

You've seen the millions people make on TV: flippers snatch up properties and flip them fast. How can you tell if the market is a seller's/flipper's market or if it's a buyer's market? There are ways to determine if the market shifts towards buyers or sellers more. For instance, once the US economy crashed in 2008, the market was considered a "buyers" market. Home prices that used to be through-the-roof suddenly reached abysmal prices and wealthy individuals with access to capital could snatch them up for the low.

Once the housing market crashes, the market becomes a buyer's market and it's very hard to flip a property for a profit. However, when the economy strengthens and money is flowing everywhere this becomes a seller's market and it's actually harder for buyers to afford the homes. Housing prices are further solidified by foreign investors trying to get a foothold in the US and investing in property. The median home value in the US is $231,000, however, in states like California it's over $500,000. A strong economy can be a negative for flippers because it's harder to find foreclosed properties at a low price. How do we determine if the market is currently a buyer's, seller's or balanced market?

The 3 Types Of Real Estate Markets

At the end of each fiscal year, statistics agencies can determine if the market was a buyer's, seller's or balanced one. Example: Gross returns on house flips are different every year. In 2018 the average gross return was 44% and it was 50% in 2017. Why the decrease in average gross returns? The economy strengthens and less people go bankrupt. This means that less properties go on the market at foreclosed prices, hence

Flipping Houses

flippers invest less because it becomes harder to find "great deals". This is neither bad or good, as an experienced flipper can find excellent deals under every possible market. The metric only displays the change in the market to help you understand why certain things happen when they happen.

#1) Seller's Market: If the market is a seller's market (a flipper is a seller too!), this means that there is a surplus in demand and a lack in supply. To imagine the best example a seller's market, think of San Francisco, CA. Each apartment that goes on sale in San Francisco is sold in a matter of days and many people enter bidding wars for the chance to purchase a living space. This is because San Francisco is a tech hub with some of the highest average salaries in the US. Despite that, the city refuses to provide building permits for high-rise buildings that would enable developers to build housing for people moving in the city. This means that living space becomes scarce and real estate and rent prices skyrocket. San Francisco is an extreme example of a seller's market, but in general if demand is high then that is a strong indicator of a seller's market.

#2) Buyer's Market: A buyer's market is when the inventory of housing surpasses that of the demand. Have you driven past empty new suburban developments that are not inhabited yet? In many cases this is an indicator of a buyer's market, as the need for housing exceeds the demand. This means that buyer's are in a superior position to sellers because they have plenty to choose from and they can even low-ball sellers for a decreased price. It is very hard to make a profit when you're in a buyer's market. Take a look at the city you're investing in. Are there many vacant new developments? Do new developments sell out fast? If the city is full of vacant properties and has a surplus of developments, it will be harder to sell a property. In the worst case scenario a property can sit on the market for a full year.

#3) **Balanced Market**: A balanced market means that inventory and demand are equalized and that for each new development there are adequate customers. The United States has been a balanced market for most of its history and the only exceptions were strong economic downshifts/recessions or micro-bubbles within certain regions that experience an economic boom. The economy of a city can have a strong impact on the real estate market and in the most extreme examples such as Detroit and San Francisco, we see either a complete collapse or an over inflation of the housing prices. In a typical balanced market, there is a 6 month advance on inventory that meets demand.

Best Market For House-Flips & Hot Markets

The best-case-scenario for a house-flipper is a seller's market. When there is a high demand for housing in a thriving city, it's a lot easier to flip a property. If no one wants to live in a city and demand for housing is low, it will be a lot harder to flip a property because selling properties is hard in general. In a balanced market, it's possible to make a healthy amount of money flipping houses.

Labor costs are affected by a shortage of workers: If there are less qualified workers to carry out tasks, the contractors will require more money. However, this depends on the local market and some markets are less impacted by labor shortages. Research your local market for contractor prices and compare them to the US average. Some markets have lower labor costs. The expenses that go into renovations will be a major factor in your bottom line.

The fastest growing cities in the US will have the highest demand for housing. The urban areas and immediate suburbs of those cities are ideal for house-flipping because they are almost always seller's markets. Think the fastest growing cities in the US are New York City and/or Los Angeles? Wrong! Per capita, the fastest growing cities are usually mid-sized cities with a strong economy. Cities such as Seattle, Austin, Denver, Omaha, Miami and Raleigh top the list as the fastest growing cities in the nation. These cities can grow as much as 15%

each 5 years. Where will all those people live? It's up to you to provide them a living space. With a strong job market and growing wages, many people can now afford a down-payment on a property. This is why "hot" real estate markets are either seller's markets or balance markets. It's up to you to take advantage and make a healthy profit on your first flip.

Chapter 3 - No Money, No Problem

Wholesaling: All You Need to Know to Get Started

Novices think they need a $120,000/yr income and a real estate license to get funding for their flips – they're wrong! We're about to distill multiple ways to acquire capital without doing it the conventional way. The spirit of house-flipping kicks in at this stage: The excitement of a research, acquisition and gathering liquid to finance your first deal. Are you ready to make your first acquisitions and research houses to buy? Are you ready to become a property owner and get the keys to your first flip? Hold on, because we're about to break down the most unconventional and secret ways to obtain funding.

The first of such methods is "wholesaling". The name "wholesale" rings bells if you ever step into the mall at Christmas - all the stores are selling merchandise at low prices to get rid of off-season stock. In real estate, wholesaling refers to virtually the same thing - getting deals off the main market. The main real estate market is the market we all see: the classified ads online, the real estate websites. Wholesaling strives to buy real estate off the main market - you can purchase your first house from wholesalers.

How To Flip A House With No Money?

It sounds like an advertising leading you on - it's not! Wholesaling can enable you to purchase properties off-market for a much lower value than they would sell on the main market. Wholesaling is low-risk because you directly contact the owner of the property to purchase their property at a discount - and once you flip it, you share the profits. This means that you never take title, i.e. you never officially become the "owner" of the property but you reap the profits at the end. You don't bear responsibility for the property and you make a spread once the property sells for a fee you agree with in advance.

Positives/Negatives Of Wholesaling

Flipping Houses

Wholesaling is the fastest method to finance and flip a property without having a lot of capital available. However, it does require more expertise and networking than a conventional house-flip.

Positives Of Wholesaling:

✓Flip houses without little/no capital.

✓No down payments or less legal fees as you never take ownership of the property.

✓Safer than conventional forms of real estate investing.

✓Ability to finance multiple deals at once.

✓Credit score is irrelevant.

Disadvantages Of Wholesaling:

✗Requires social acuity, networking and knowledge about the whole process.

✗Must seek out investors who will bankroll the deals.

✗Must plan out an exit strategy for a property you don't own.

✗If you don't finance the deal you will make less than the investor.

How Wholesaling Works

Wholesaling is house-flipping WITHOUT taking ownership of the property. Wholesalers discover a house seller who agrees to partner with them and allow them to acquire the house at a low price. This effectively makes the wholesaler act as the "middle man" between the owner and the future buyer. This is ideal for beginners because it decreases the risk of things going wrong and them being stuck with a house. Wholesaling is ideal for beginners, however, new wholesalers should consult real estate attorneys for all assignment contingencies. It's on you to select how much you'll charge in "assignment fees" which are your profits for acting as the middleman financier.

Flipping Houses

How To Determine If Wholesaling Is For You

If you have the know-how to seek-out investors who can put up the initial money for renovations and you know how to find property owners who would agree to a flip deal, you are ideal for wholesaling. This method is perfect for people who like to network and can put people together on a deal. Start on Linkedin to build local connections to people involved in house-flipping finance and real-estate. Your job as a wholesaler is to learn your local market, develop connections, know about the cost of repairs and cut a deal with the investors.

Essentially, you don't need any money to start wholesaling! You can network with financiers who will put up the money for the house-purchase and the renovations, find a person willing to sell their house at a discount without taking title, and flip the house. You will have to carry out the same repairs as if you financed and repaired the house yourself, but you will be taking other people's money and directing it for the highest investment-profit ROI.

Calculating Profit For Wholesaling

To operate as wholesaler, you must develop a wholesale mindset - you can't apply the same principles as a regular flipper because many properties won't work as wholesales. As a rule of thumb, you should seek to identify properties that can work as wholesales and the following formula applies:

ARV * 70% - repair cost - your fee = Offer you give.

Take out your calculator now! Let's make an example at an average $125,000 house that requires $25,000 in repairs for a total re-sell value of $150,000. What would your final profit be and how much should you offer the house owner to make that profit?

$150,000 (after-repair value) * 70% - $25,000 (repair cost) - $15,000 (your wholesaling fee) = $65,000.

Your maximum offer for this house should be $65,000. If you want to close it instantly you should consider lowering your wholesaling fee to $10,000 to offer the property-owner $70,000 for the house. In both cases, you're free to decide the wholesaling fee based on how much you think the owner would agree to. If the property owners are open to negotiation, you should set a higher fee. If they act stingy and refuse to sell, offer them a lower wholesaling fee. The final offer will determine how much you can take home: if you offer less, you will take more profit. If you offer more, you will take less profit. Determine if the profit on a wholesale is worth all the effort you'll put in the property.

Warning: Research the property owner to determine if the property owners owe too much before you offer them a deal, because in many cases they won't give you a good deal if they're in severe debt. Good deals are possible if both parties see a profit, not at the expense of the other party.

Once you've identified a deal you have to sign a separate "wholesaling contract" which will entitle you to fix up the property and ultimately sell it for a profit - once it's sold the previous owner has to move out. Real estate lawyers who specialize in this law practice can ensure the escrow funds and transactions are carried out in an efficient manner. Wholesale contracts are taken up by real estate professionals who flip properties for a living - professionals like you. It's your job to identify eligible properties, negotiate a deal with the seller, renovate the property and sell it for a profit.

How to Get a Hard Money Loan

Think you need to spend months guaranteeing the bank you will pay back your loans? Are you struggling to gather all the evidence your bank loan manager asks before he approves your loan? What about time - do you have all the paperwork but the bank still takes months to approve your loans? Hard money loans help you get around that. Your loan can be approved in as little as 7 days and the average approval time is less than 10 days. This allows the lender to analyze the property and determine if it will make a profit before approving your loan. "Fix and flip" lending is how thousands of properties are sold each month, and this lending enables flippers who are always on the lookout for the next deal to finance their next property. Don't wait to finish your current project before you gather more finances - you can apply for multiple loans at once and fix up multiple properties. While you're working on your current property, you could line up the next one.

Hard money loans are real-estate loans for flippers who require fast access to capital without consulting banks. Banks have rigid approval procedures that take weeks or even months - hard money loans are issued within days, effectively allowing flippers to capitalize on current investments while bankrolling multiple properties at once. Hard money loans are for flippers who want to invest in multiple properties and require fast approval procedures. If you want to flip multiple properties at once without wasting months before financing new properties, this loan type is for you.

Sound too good to be true? Hard money loans do have higher interest rates but they cater to a certain demographic of flippers who can afford to pay higher interest rates because the speed makes up for the surcharge on interest. Time is of the essence here: The faster you flip your property, the less you pay in interest. If you can flip properties fast you will reap higher rewards. Hard money loans, also known as "fix and flip" loans allow you to get in and out of the market fast and secure the capital you need to renovate and sell a property.

Pro Tip: Prepare your property acquisition documents in advance as "fix and flip" loans require detailed documentation to expedite approval. This part takes the most and once your loan is approved (usually within days) you can purchase the property and start working.

Advantages Of Hard Money Loans:

✓Only 10% down-payment required: Can finance 90% of the property acquisition cost and 100% of all renovations.

✓No upfront contracts or costs pre-approval.

✓Average approval time of 7-10 days (45 days for conventional bank loans).

Flipping Houses

✓All types of real estate accepted (houses, condos, commercial properties, etc).

✓Can apply with bad credit history, past bankruptcies or back taxes owed.

Disadvantages of hard-money loans:

✗4-5% higher interest than conventional loans. The average interest rate is 5-8%.

Hard Money Loans VS Conventional Bank Loans

The main advantage of hard money loans is that they approve loans based on the asset in question - not the borrower. The conventional bank will analyze your personal employment, finances, job history, credit score and account for your personal liability. Hard money lenders only care for the property: They want to know the property will flip and sell. The entire focus is on the property. Hard money loans are catered to flippers and provide coverage for all flipper's needs: purchase costs, closing costs, legal costs, permit costs, and renovations. In hard money loans, the all-around financing is called "asset based underwriting" - this is the main advantage over conventional loans. Hard money loans are available to people with bad or limited credit histories, as the focus is put on the deals themselves, not the person.

Wouldn't it be great if all banks only looked at your deals and decided to finance projects based on which one seems most profitable instead of digging in your personal history? This is the essence of hard money loans - while banks would consider it risky to invest in the house-flipping business, fix-and-flip loans thrive on volatile investments such as flipping because they bankroll the entire project and know that the property is guaranteed to make a profit (based on market research and other metrics conducive to the ARV of the property). They also don't exclude people with a history of bad credit. Even if your current credit score is good, a bank will outright refuse you if you had a bankruptcy under your belt. Asset-lending is secured by the collateral and the lenders are not in danger as they can acquire the property if you fail to flip it and make payments. However, they are also open to finance all your endeavors and help you gather the finances you need to make the property shine.

Pro Tip: Time is your main ally in hard money loans. If a property looks too shabby and your intuition tells you it's going to take months to fix it - ditch it. You need a solid property that you can flip within a few weeks by upgrading basics such as the bedrooms, bathrooms, kitchens and/or paint. The faster you get rid of the property, the less you pay in interest. This is further expedited if you have your documents in place, as your loan can be approved in as little as a week.

How To Get A Hard Money Loan?

Start by gathering all your paperwork related to the property. This includes your current finances, the property value, research, calculations in terms of repairs and your profit expectations. The lenders will ask you for documentation and might inquire as to your personal history as an investor. Answer questions honestly! If you've never flipped a property, tell them this is your first flip. Preparing the documentation and gaining approval takes the most time - make sure you're prepared in advance.

What Are The Interest Rates?

The interest rates on hard money loans are on average 4% higher than on regular bank loans - this is actually a great deal considering the speed and low personal standards they impose for applying for a loan. In essence, you're paying a 4-5% premium on the interest for faster access to capital which enables you to finance multiple properties at once. The applications also require a lot less underwriting. The focus is put on the property itself: If you can prove the property will be profitable for the lenders, they will secure you a loan.

Is the process that much faster? Why pay 4% more in interest when you can wait for a bank loan? The answer is simple: If you want speed, you pay a premium for the privilege. Banks are reliable institutions for financing properties, but banks will analyze your credit history and the average approval for a bank loan is 45 days (close to 2 months). If you can wait 2 months for a loan to be approved, you should opt for the lower interest rates of a bank. In essence, banks are better for people who have excellent credit ratings and plan to flip very few properties each year. Hard money loans are for people who want to flip a dozen properties every year and don't want to wait months for approval on each loan.

The biggest advantage of "fix-and-flip" loans is that lenders understand flippers. Lenders know that the essence of house-flipping is about the asset itself and they invest based on the deal - not about who you are and how your past divorce caused you to go bankrupt. If you present a great deal such as a fixable property that requires little renovations but has potential of selling, you are almost guaranteed to receive a hard money loan. If you have previous experience flipping properties, your loans could be approved in less than a week.

Flipping Houses With No Money Using Private Investors

Are you scared to approach financiers who would bankroll your property? Worry not - we'll teach you how to locate private lenders to finance your property. Private lending is in essence reaching out to people who have money to finance your flip when you don't have money. A private lender could technically be your relative or your father in law. However, in most cases private lenders are established businessmen who invest their assets in local, high-risk investments. Private lenders are individual partners who bankroll the flip of a property - this type of lending is similar to "fix-and-flip" loans but you deal with individuals in person instead of financial institutions.

Private lending is a form of obtaining capital from individuals who specialize in lending to flippers. Lenders who bankroll properties tend to be wealthy and established individuals that you can reach out to and obtain funding in person. What's in it for them? They get a cut at the end of each flip, and their cut is usually bigger than that of bank loans. Private lenders don't care about your credit score but they want you to have a track record of flipping properties before they write you a 6-

figure check for your newest flip. To secure their investment, lenders make flippers sign a "first deed of trust" agreement (mortgage) which means their money is secured by a hard asset (the property purchased).

Who Is Qualified For A Private Loan?

Each individual who want to flip properties can reach out to investors for a private loan. There are no minimum finances or minimum credit scores required. However, to get an investor the main "qualifier" for you would be your past experience and track record. Dealing with private lenders is only recommended for people who have flipped at least one property, because many of them won't engage with novices. They want to know their investment is secure before they put down a six-figure payment for your new property. Your chances of being successful with private lenders will be exponentially higher if you have a history of flipping properties in the past.

Pro Tip: Start with a regular bank loan and flip your first property using low-risk bank loans. Once you've flipped your first property, most fix-and-flip lenders and private-money lenders will approve your loans. You will then be able to flip multiple properties at the same time (as you already have a 'track record' of flipping properties).

What Are Private Lenders?

Private lenders aren't always retired wealthy individuals who you meet at the Country Club – you can now find private lenders on LinkedIn. Private lenders can also be "investment groups" or "partnership groups" that finance real estate deals; this will depend on your city/state and financial options available. In most cases private lenders provide direct finances: Whatever amount you estimate you'll need for the acquisition and repair costs, they'll bankroll it. However, they also collect their cut which you'll have to negotiate at the start. The main advantage with private lenders is that many times they won't even ask you for a down payment, but they only trust flippers with a past track record.

How To Get A Private Loan?

Flipping Houses

This is where the fun part kicks in - you don't even need a down payment with private lenders. It's possible to combine two funding sources: One that will finance the purchase/repair price (but ask for a down payment) and another lender who will finance the down payment for the original loan. It's possible to obtain funding from two lenders who will finance your deal, and at the end of the sale distribute the profits equally and accordingly to each investor. What you have is "sweat equity": You identify an attractive real-estate deal and you carry out the rehab and selling process on your own. The lenders use their resource to finance your purchase.

Private lending can work in multiple ways, however, the two most common are the following:

1) Two partners join together: One handles the financing (supplies the funding) and the other discovers a deal, carries out repairs and sells the property.

2) Three partners join together: One handles the financing, the other handles the down payment for the financing and the third (you) handles the property.

How To Find Qualified Private Investors

To make private deals run smoothly, you will have to identify whether the person you're doing business with is qualified to provide the financing for your flip. The following 3 traits are what separate good investors from bad investors:

1. Access to wealth/resources. A private lender has to be a wealthy individual who invests in many flippers like yourself, and this shouldn't be their first investment. The profile of private lenders is usually established, middle aged or older business owners.

2. Transparent communications. Private lenders will be eager to discuss the details of the acquisition and all the construction/repair costs, including the final sale price. They will be transparent about the purchase and tell you exactly how much they can finance and what their cut is at the end.

3. Separation of roles. The investor has to realize your sweat equity and the amount of effort/work you put into the property - this way there is no confusion as to the scope of work involved or how much you deserve at the end of the sale.

There are many ways to source out private lenders, but the best way to start is to find lenders located in your area.

Researching Lenders In Your Area

The best way to start is by networking: Attend real-estate events and seminars and meet people in "the business". They will be able to put you in touch with investors and you should be able to meet them in person at these events. However, if you don't have time to network or don't know how to you can also look up local county records for all properties that will include the closed rate, the interest and the lender's contact details. Look up who lent out in your vicinity within the last 3-6 months as those lenders are likely active on the market.

Once you've accumulated a list of investors/lenders, you should directly reach out to them. Most lenders leave their email, but you can make a stronger impression by cold-calling them and pitching them a deal.

Example: "Hello, is this lender [name]? My name is [your name] and I see that you've lent out money for this project on 94 Street, Nashville. My company does fix-up projects and I'm calling to see if you're interested in one more of these deals".

There are no rules as to how the conversation is supposed to flow – this is about your personal relationship with the lender. The wisest option is to talk about how you flipped houses in the past to get the investor comfortable with how you do business. Do everything you can to establish rapport and make them comfortable by discussing their projects, the scope of deals they do, their town, family or even sports. The more comfortable they feel with you as a person, the more willing they'll be to finance your projects.

Chapter 4 - Choosing the Right Property

Key Factors For Choosing The Right Location

Location, location, location! People would rather invest $250,000 in a house in a good neighborhood than spend $150,000 on a house in a bad neighborhood (even if they can afford both!). Have you ever driven to a friend's place and thought "Wow, this is a good area?". If the roads are in good shape, houses look maintained and there are nearby amenities you assume that it's a good, safe neighborhood. How do you feel when you drive past a neighborhood with bad houses, shanty roads full of potholes, unlit street lights and bulletproof-sealed convenience stores? You instantly want to get out! House-flipping is not about choosing the first $30,000 "deal" that comes your way. Certain neighborhoods always have low property values for a reason and they're much more prone to crime. Once you arrive at the location of your flip and you get a personal taste of the neighborhood, you can immediately identify the class of neighborhood it is. This is why you must always investigate properties by visiting them instead of relying on online research.

Classes Of Neighborhoods

There are 4 classes of neighborhoods in real estate: A-class, B-class, C-class and D-class. Similar to a school grading system, in real estate neighborhoods arc rated based on property value, location and overall condition. Think of it this way: The most desirable neighborhoods are the class A neighborhoods. The least desirable ones are the class D neighborhoods, and class D includes abandoned properties.

Class A neighborhoods are the kind of houses every family wishes to live in: They're the epitome of the American Dream. Class B and C neighborhoods are more or less "average" neighborhood: Class B/C are slightly outdated, many of them are in bad shape but they're generally safe and habitable. Class D neighborhoods are crime-ridden, the houses are in bad shape, and they command low property values. We avoid class D neighborhoods for the purpose of house-flipping because even a renovated property in those neighborhoods can sit on the market for long. For the purpose of maximizing profits, we focus on class B and class C neighborhoods where we can snatch up properties on the low and renovate them.

Pro Tip: There is no government organization that "officially" classifies neighborhoods. You must differentiate classes based on your own knowledge and intuition.

1) Class A Neighborhoods

Class A neighborhoods are new affluent and safe neighborhoods. Those include the "elite" mansions and high-HOA communities, but they also include very new developments. Have you driven past a spanking new, shiny suburb that has all-new properties, access to good schools, security patrols, restaurants, and other first-class amenities? That is your typical class A neighborhood. Many of them are new and built in the last 10 years, which is why the maintenance is very low and the property value per square foot is the highest. Typically interiors consist of high-tech amenities such as granite countertops, "smart" curtains, hardwood floors, expensive finishes and pools. Class A neighborhoods make good rental investments, but they are not the best for flipping because many of them are already "renovated" and the flipper will have to fork out serious cash to upgrade those houses.

2) Class B Neighborhoods

Class B is actually similar to class A – Class B houses have the same amenities and high-quality infrastructure, but they tend to be older. Class B neighborhoods are safe with access to good schools, hospitals and shopping options. Class B neighborhoods are typically populated by middle-income citizens and they have very few citizens who struggle and live paycheck to paycheck. The typical house in a class B neighborhood is 30 years old and in good shape. If any repairs are required they will typically be lower than those of Class C and D neighborhoods. In essence, a class B neighborhood is a slightly older and downgraded version of a class A neighborhood.

3) Class C Neighborhoods

Class C neighborhoods are lower-income neighborhoods where the infrastructure tends to be outdated, the houses are old and in bad shape and the residents are typically low-income. Many residents of class C neighborhoods will be on government subsidies and struggling to get by. Class C neighborhoods are not as unsafe as class D neighborhoods, but their safety is a lot worse compared to prime Class A and B neighborhoods. Typical signs of a class C neighborhood include bad maintenance of lawns, extra security around houses, pawn shops/liquor stores, cash checking businesses, weapons stores, etc. Most houses in class C neighborhoods are at least 30+ years old and can be over 50 years old. They will require heavy repairs, but the price difference between these homes and Class B homes can be significant and worth a flip.

4) Class D Neighborhoods

Class D neighborhoods don't exist in every city but they are easy to recognize: Abandoned buildings, decaying old infrastructure, unlit streets, gang presence, visible drug sales and constant police presence. In many cases police is afraid to enter class D neighborhoods themselves. Even public infrastructure such as schools can be abandoned with squatters inside and all working convenience stores have bulletproof windows and armed employees who work behind 3 foot glass. In many cases, class D neighborhoods should be avoided even if they're extraordinarily cheap. Once the renovations are carried out, it will be harder to sell or even rent out the property because it's in a dangerous area. Unless you specialize in flipping class D properties and don't feel threatened by the areas, you should generally avoid flipping properties in such locations.

Factors That Increases Property Value

The following things need to be checked on your list to ensure the property you flip will command a high resell value:

✓**Parks/green spaces**. If the property is located near a park or a green space such as woods/hiking trails this can increase property value up to 20%.

✓**School districts**. If the property is located in a good public school district, this can increase property values by 20%. Surveyed buyers say they would pay up to 20% for a home in a good school district.

✓**Medical facilities**. If the property is located close to hospitals this will increase the property value.

✓**Maintenance levels**. The maintenance level of the neighborhood such as road condition, sidewalks, street lights, cleanliness, maintained yards, etc, can increase the property value significantly. In HOA communities this is handled by a single institution and residents only pay monthly fees.

✓**Recreation/shopping**. If the property is located near restaurants, shopping malls, recreation centers and other entertainment options this will increase property value.

✓**Walkability**. If the home is located in a walkable area where clients can walk to convenience stores, this increases property value. If a car is required for a trip to the store, this can negatively impact the property value.

✓**Public transportation (only for urban areas).** In urban areas access to public transportation such as bus stops and metro stations can increase property value.

Factors That Decrease Property Value

What are "hidden" value killers that sellers don't advertise on realtor ads? What if you see an epic deal and you're ready to put down a payment, only to learn there's a reason why it's that cheap? The following things can decrease property value significantly:

✗**Airports**. If the property is located next to an airport it will have constant noise from airplanes taking off and landing. Airplanes are noise machines and flights usually land 24/7 which makes rest impossible.

✘**Train station/metro station**. Trains produce a squeaky noise and if a property is located near a train station or a metro, the owners will be able to hear trains passing by the whole day.

✘**Fire department/PD**. If the property is located near a fire department or a police station, they will witness activity and patrol cars making noise around the clock - this decreases the value of a property.

✘**Highways nearby**. If the property is located next to a major highway the passing cars will produce noise 24/7 which decreases the quality of life for residents. Many local governments put up noise barriers on highways but that usually doesn't block out all the noise.

✘**Nightlife establishments**. If the property is located near nightlife establishments such as clubs/bars this can affect the quality of life for residents and lower property value.

Noise pollution is the #1 property-price killer because it decreases the quality of life for people residing in houses near noisy establishments.

Take Action - Visit The Property!

When you research your neighborhood, online data is does not cut it – you must visit the property yourself. Don't just drive to the property in a rush! Take a spin across the street and analyze the nearby streets. Does the neighborhood feel safe, are there people walking around, are children playing freely, are the street lights working, are the lawns trimmed, are the houses in good shape, are there local schools and amenities? These are all things you will discover in less than one hour of observing a neighborhood. It will give the last bit of reassurance you need before you put down a house payment.

Features to Look For & Features to Avoid in Property

What is the difference between buying a cheap property and renovating it vs. buying a normal-priced property and renovating it? Are you falling to the temptation of buying the first $30,000 house you see in your city? The price cannot make up for things you can't fix –

Flipping Houses

it's important to analyze the features first. Here's how most novices mess up:

Expectation: You will buy a $30,000 house and spend $50,000 renovating it and you'll conclude your first flip. You're now a profitable house-flipper!

Reality: The repairs now take too long, you can't do anything without a permit, you wait for inspector meetings, your repairs are delayed and it takes forever. You lose money!

How do you identify properties that take little cosmetic fixes which you can renovate in a month, without waiting for inspections, permits and dealing with other legal hurdles? These are things you have to look out for before you purchase a property. In general, you want to avoid projects that seem too "difficult" to add or change anything. You want to focus on simple cosmetic upgrades. If the property is too far run down, it will be impossible to fix unless you spend months on it. If the property is in good shape, you can get away with as little as a few cosmetic upgrades such as the paint-job. If the property is in decent shape and has good features, you'll find it easy to fix and sell on the market. If the property is hard to fix, it will be impossible to fix, lose you time on permits and sit on the market longer.

Pro Tip: The golden rule of identifying properties is to find "easy to fix" properties. If a property looks easy to fix, you should snatch it instantly. If the property is too far gone, seek out better properties.

Factors That Sell A Property

The following are the most sought-after features in a property. Prior to putting down a payment on a house, you should find one that ticks all boxes or come close to the ideal:

✓**Large bedrooms**. The best-selling houses are houses with 3 bedrooms. That is a typical American house. Seek out a house with a large master bedroom that can house a king sized bed and has space to walk around it. The secondary bedrooms should be large enough to accommodate a queen sized bed or two small beds. The first thing people look for is the number of bedrooms - the more bedrooms you have the better. Find houses that have spacious master bedrooms.

✓**Multiple bathrooms**. As a rule-of-thumb the house should have at least 1 bathroom for each floor. If you have a house with 2 floors and there's only one bedroom, move on. The same holds true for half-bathrooms, each floor has to have a full bathroom. This is valuable for families that have multiple members. If a house has more bathrooms, the owner will be able to host parties and when their house is "full" they will need multiple bathrooms. Do you wonder why big mansions have 10-15 bathrooms? They need the space for parties where 200-300 people gather in the mansion at once.

✓**Navigable layout**. If you enter the house and you have a bathroom in front of you, you will not have a good impression of a home. The home has to feel "open" and easy to navigate without tight spaces. A bad layout can be fixed if you hire contractors to tear down the walls, but the ideal property is one that doesn't need any walls torn down. Popular layouts include "open kitchen" layouts that have a mini-bar attached to the living room. This makes for easy entertaining.

✓**Garage space**. It goes without saying that a house must have at least a 1-car garage to park the car - people don't like parking in front of their house unless they have to. The ideal garage is a two-car garage. Unless you're going for a luxury property, there is no need to upgrade the garage for more than 2 spaces.

Factors That Delay A Property Sale

Many things can go wrong with your property: You have to do extensive renovations that can be both time-consuming and expensive. This will hurt your budget and extend the time you need until a complete renovation ensues. The local council might require permits for some renovations you have to make - this will mean inspectors arriving at your property, reviewing your renovations, issuing permits that might take forever and then delays in repairs. This will hurt your bottom line and cost you a fortune. How to avoid that? Look for the following signs that hinder renovations and house sales:

Flipping Houses

✗Structural issues. Is the roof of the house unstable and will require a replacement? Are there holes in the foundation of the house? Are the floors uneven? Are there cracks all over the place? All these will require a lot of time and experienced contractors to fix. If the house has structural issues - ditch it.

✗Outdated designs. Many houses that were built for older generations are undesirable for today's ones. **Example**: Low ceilings are undesirable and high ceilings over 9 feet are now desirable. Narrow kitchens are a big no no! The modern American wants a wide kitchen where they can move freely and cook their dinner. Any closed-off spaces, low bearing walls and ceilings will be hard to sell.

✗Uneven bed/bath ratios. If the house has 4 bedrooms but only 1 bathroom, this means the house was not designed carefully. Seek out houses that have at least 1 bathroom for each 2 bedrooms. If you buy a 4 bedroom house, it should have at least 2 bathrooms or 1.5 bathrooms if you compromise. The bedroom-bathroom ratio should be even and not skewed in favor of bedrooms.

✗ Inaccessible rooms. Houses with bad designs will be "closed off" i.e. you won't be able to enter one room without entering another. The ideal house has "open" rooms that can be accessed from main lobbies. **Example**: The master bathroom is only accessible through the master bedroom. This means everyone who wants to go to the bathroom will have to enter the bedroom first. This is a bad design.

'Easy' Repairs That Increase Property Value

Want to make upgrades you can't go wrong with? There are upgrades for all levels - a new bathroom could cost $10,000. A change in the light system can only cost $1000. All repairs depend on what you're trying to fix. In general, you want to focus on cosmetic repairs to increase the value of the property. If your focus is on structural repairs, you will over-spend and your whole budget will be allocated to fixing problems that don't exist on normal properties. The following repairs can reap massive financial rewards:

Flipping Houses

✓**Paint-jobs**. The go-to fix for every property is a new paint-job. Some paint-jobs will be easy but others might get costly depending on the state of the walls. Start by painting the walls in neutral colors such as white or grey. The paint will cover up any blemishes or patching holes in the walls. This is the easiest upgrade for every property that can boost property value. The exterior paint will depend on what is suitable for the property and neighborhood: Neutral colors are a go-to for exteriors.

✓**New floors and carpets**. Each floor in the house can be replaced with a new, modern hardwood floor. This can be a costly upgrade but it can make a significant difference in the impression people have of a property. New carpets can also add a "premium" feeling to the property, and many of them are affordable. Carpets should be in a neutral color as very light carpets (example: white carpets) will attract dirt and make it visible.

✓**Light fixtures and ceiling fans**. Ceiling fans are very desirable and increase the value of a property - almost 90% of people want a ceiling fan in their home. Light fixtures can be upgraded to modern LED fixtures that operate on "smart" control and can set the vibe of the environment for relaxation. Simple light upgrades can make the home feel modern and sleek.

✓**Interior upgrades**. The interior can change the perception a person has of a house. Interior upgrades such as modern furniture can bring an outdated home to the 21st century. Popular interiors include minimalistic couches, glass/wooden tables, plasma screens and many interiors come in a "package" which helps you revamp the property at once by picking the most suitable one.

✓**Updating infrastructure**. The infrastructure of the house such as the plumbing fixtures which are visible can be updated to newer ones at a low cost. New plumbing fixtures have modern finishes that look great and add a "neat home" feeling.

✓**Landscaping upgrades**. The exterior of the house can improve the "curb appeal" (the first impression people get as they drive by the house). This includes repairing a patchy lawn/making it greener, adding planters, power-washing the whole home, upgrading the entry door, etc. Landscaping will improve the appeal of a house for pictures, making it more upscale and premium looking.

✓**Kitchen/bathroom upgrades**. These are the most expensive upgrades as those two require special treatment compared to living rooms and bedrooms. Most customers expect stainless steel kitchen appliances: fridges, stoves, microwaves, blenders, etc. Simple upgrades such as "smart fridges" can cost thousands of dollars. The upgrades you choose should be set based on your budget.

✓**Window upgrades**. If the windows are outdated, replacing them with new windows can improve the aesthetics of the home. New windows can also increase the energy efficiency of the house, preserving heat in the winter and keeping the home cool in the summer.

Golden Rules for Picking Property

You have $150,000 to invest and your city has hundreds of houses to buy. Even after you narrow your search down to sub $75,000< properties you can still pick out many. How do you choose which one is the right one? How do you know which house will "flip" out of hundreds of houses? The key to selection is to make your calculations in advance! You have to take in account many things: neighborhood, structural integrity, asking price, renovation costs, etc, and you must do it all at once! Many novice flippers barely make a profit or even lose money on their first flip, because they ignore the pre-calculations necessary to be successful in house-flipping. Why would you spend weeks or months toiling with a property only to be left with a miniscule property? It's possible to estimate the profit margins well in advance of purchasing a property (unless you're buying a foreclosed home which you can't see).

Flipping Houses

Golden Rule #1: The Location Is 50% Of The Flip

In each home flip, the location is 50% of the value and the house is 50% of the value. Location matters as much as the actual house. A property can be in the worst condition: Ran down, outdated, uninhabitable. However, if the property is located in a desirable area (proximity to schools, restaurants, shopping venues and/or scenery) someone will snatch it based on that fact. The location is the most vital bit of research you have to do. Fortunately in this day and age we can analyze houses on Google Street View without ever setting foot on the actual property. Mapping technology and online tools allow us to narrow down a list of properties before visiting in person.

There are two things that determine a good location: Scenery and infrastructure. If the house is located near a large body of water, this can dramatically increase the price of the property. Example: An ocean-view house in Malibu might sell for $8M and a highway-view house in the same neighborhood might sell for $4M. This is half price, only because one provides a direct view of the ocean. The closer the house is to oceans, lakes and rivers - the higher the property value. People prefer well-lit houses with views and access to natural light.

If the house has views of mountains, cities or water - it will command higher property rates. However, most houses are located in good-old suburbs. In this case, the only thing that determines home value is infrastructure: State of roads, build quality of houses, maintenance levels, school districts, medical facilities, proximity to amenities and safety. The better a neighborhood, the more expensive the average house is going to be. All properties can be flipped! Million-dollar homes in the hills and ran-down shacks in the ghetto can be flipped on the same principles. The home you need is something in between!

Golden Rule #2) Choose The Worst House In The Best Neighborhood

Based on what you can afford, always opt for the highest-tier neighborhood with the newest houses. Why focus on the better neighborhoods in your budget? They will likely have newer designs

Flipping Houses

that are easy to upgrade and even the worst house in a good neighborhood will be better than an average house in a bad neighborhood. Good neighborhoods will have access to good schools, medical facilities, restaurants, shopping malls, police/PD, highway networks and other first-class amenities that make for a good life.

Pro Tip: No matter how much money you invest in renovations, it will never change the location of the home. Buyers don't want to live in a high-crime area. Pick out the best neighborhood you can find and buy a house in that neighborhood based on your budget.

Golden Rule #3) Buy Cookie Cutter Homes

Always opt for the most average/neutral looking cookie-cutter homes you can find. Why buy that "unique" property? That will exclude a large part of the potential customer pool. If anything feels "odd" about a property (such as the roof has a guitar imprint because the owner was a guitarist) and the property was customized to the demands of a previous owner, avoid it. The property has to look similar to properties in the immediate area. Once clients visit the property they will also look at the properties across the street. If they notice yours stands out, they won't buy it. Even though it sounds harsh in practice, cookie-cutter homes sell fast. Seek out the most average home you can get with nothing unique about it and flip that.

The same applies for your next door neighbors! Make sure there aren't eye-sores in your immediate area. If potential buyers like the home but the home across the street is in bad shape, they will be put off. Does your neighbor dump garbage in front of their house? Do they have their cars parked all over the lawn? Is there a giant boat sticking out their garage? The state of your neighbor's property can affect the value of yours. In essence, you need to find a "normal" home in a "normal" neighborhood. This ensures the home will appeal to the highest number of customers and won't stay on the market for too long.

Golden Rule #4: Avoid Outdated Constructions

Remember the year 1978 - this is the cutoff year for every property you want to purchase. All homes before 1978 used lead based paint and the US "Environmental Protection Agency" changed the paint regulations in that year and which means they consider the possibility that all homes built before 1978 still have lead based paint. In practice, the local government will harass you for documentation on every renovation once they schedule audits. You carefully select pre-approved paints that this will increase your construction costs and make the approval procedure time-consuming. There are certain "guidelines" for all houses built before 1978 that make simple cosmetic fixes like paint-jobs impossible. In addition, the government can fine owners up to $30,000 for not adhering to those regulations.

The layouts of old homes are also a deal-breaker for most new buyers. **Example**: Many old homes have rooms that lead to other rooms and certain rooms are inaccessible from the main lobby. New buyers prefer homes that have "open" floor plans in which each room is accessible independent of other rooms and open-kitchens are also popular. In the past kitchen areas were closed-off with tight space. Current kitchen areas are open and/or adjacent to the living room for easy entertainment.

Golden Rule #5: Flip The House In 3 Months Or Less

The more time spent on renovations, the more it will hurt your wallet. Invest in houses that would take a maximum of 3 months to flip: 1 month for the paperwork and acquisition, 1 month for the renovations and 1 month for the flip. Once you've narrowed down your neighborhoods, the selection should depend on which house would take the least time to fix. If the house seems like it would take more than 1-2 months to renovate, forget about it! If you can renovate a house in less than a month using simple cosmetic fixes (paint, interior decor, landscaping, etc) go for it. If the house has structural problems, each problem could take a month on its own. As a flipper you want to get in and out of deals as fast as possible, leaving you with a sizable profit on each flip.

The longer your house stays on the market the more money you'll have to spend for HOA, insurance, utilities, property taxes, landscaping and/or takeover fees. Houses less than 2000 sq feet are the easiest to renovate because you only renovate 2-3 bedrooms at a time. If the house is large the repairs will take longer and they are more extensive, even if you're only making minor cosmetic repairs.

How to Calculate Your Net Profit

The average gross profit for a house flip in the US is $60,000 - this is before Uncle Sam takes home your income taxes and capital gains taxes apply on assets you've held for less than one year. To calculate the net profit on each flip, you must account for all costs of acquisition: The property purchase, renovation, carrying costs (property taxes, insurance, HOA, utilities, landscape maintenance, closing costs/realtor costs) and then make a deposit on a property. Then, you have to calculate your own individual income taxes based on your state and income levels which you must calculate on your own. For the purpose of this demonstration, we will take an average house flip and calculate all the important costs while explaining what each cost signifies.

Budgeting is essential to successfully flipping the house. The "net" profit in house-flipping refers to the final profit you make after the property is sold - not the income taxes that follow. For example, if your profit at the end of the sale is $40,000 this is considered your "net profit". It is the money that you're left with after you subtract all your renovation expenses, carrying costs and realtor fees.

The Spreadsheet Of Costs

- **Property cost.** This is the largest cost - in many cases the property acquisition price will be 60-70% of your total budget, depending on the renovations you want to carry out. You can lower your purchase price by seeking out deals and foreclosures in your immediate area. Once banks foreclose a property they want to "get rid of it" fast and they sell at under market-value. The less you spend on the property, the more money you'll be left with at the end.
- **Renovation costs.** This will include all the renovations you want to make: paint jobs, interior upgrades, tearing down walls, exterior/landscaping upgrades and more. The renovation costs include

the materials required, labor costs and all other surcharges that might arise.

- **Maintenance costs**. Maintenance cost are sometimes referred to as "carrying" costs because one has to pay monthly maintenance on the property including mortgage, utilities, insurance, HOA, and property taxes. The longer your property stays on the market, the more you'll have to pay in maintenance costs.
- **Realtor fees**. Realtors take care of the photography, marketing and listing of the property. They also meet clients first-hand and sell the property in person. Realtors typically charge 5% but many will accept 4% if you negotiate. If you skip realtors you'll have to sell the property yourself.

How To Calculate Your Net Profits

We use math to estimate the net profits once the property is sold. For the purpose of this demonstration we'll analyze one class-B property that we want to sell for $140,000.

Property price: $85,000

Renovation costs: $15,000

Buying closing costs: $1000

Selling closing costs: $5000

Taxes: $1000

The formula: $85,000 (property acquisition) + $22,000 (renovations + fees) = $33,000

NET PROFIT: $33,000

Once we take the final selling price of $140,000 and we subtract our total costs, we end up with a net profit of $33,000. The $33,000 figure is the net profit you're left with at the end of each sale. **Note**: There are separate buying costs at the start that include realtor fees on your end. There are also closing fees at the end that include your realtor fees and

Flipping Houses

the buyer's realtor fees. If we estimate a moderate $15,000 budget for cosmetic upgrades, this amounts to $33,000 in pure profit.

The IRS taxes your flipping individually you'll have to pay at the end of each fiscal year, but it's impossible to calculate this in advance because if you aim to flip 3-4 properties a year, you'll be taxed on the combined profit from your flips. Most house flips are taxed under "capital gains" taxes which is a sub-category of income taxes that applies once someone sells an asset. For example, if a person inherits a $2M property and decides to sell it, the IRS will collect capital gains tax on the sale. If someone sells a business, capital gains taxes apply too. The same applies for your combined profits. House-flippers pay "short term capital gains" taxes for assets that they've held under a year. Short term capital gains taxes are almost 100% higher than those of long-term capital gains taxes (assets you've held for over a year). The lowest capital gains tax bracket is 10% for profits under $10,000 and it progressively increases up to 37% on profits over $500,000. Once you've calculated your total profits for the year, you can calculate your net profits based on the tax bracket and total profits.

Chapter 5 - It's All About Value

The 4 Best Value-Boosting Renovations

The magic number for renovating real estate is $40,000 - if you have $40,000 to spend you can install the highest quality bathrooms, kitchens and exterior renovations. You can revamp the home for half the price at $20,000 or even less - $10,000 if you're careful and do many things yourself. The two biggest value-boosters for a home are the kitchen and the bathroom. Those two alone can upgrade the value of a home by $50,000-100,000. We're talking big-revamps now! The big overhauls cost the most and can increase home value significantly. The kitchen is the heart of the home and making small adjustments to the kitchen area can significantly boost the value of the property. If this is your first flip, focus on the big 3: kitchen, bathroom and living room. There are many "small" upgrades which you can make such as paint jobs, light fixtures, landscaping, interior upgrades, etc, but most money in flipping is spent in the kitchen and bathroom. If you purchase a brand-new bathroom with the highest quality materials it can run up to $20,000 easily. There are ways to get that down by making small upgrades (which we'll distill below).

Let's talk numbers: The kitchen provides the highest ROI in terms of value. You will on average see a 3x return on your investment in the kitchen. **Example**: If you spend $5000 the buyer is going to think you spent $15,000. The bathroom also has a huge multiplier. For each $5000 you spend on a bathroom, the buyer will think you spent $10,000. If you spend $20,000 on a bathroom the buyer will think you spent $40,000. Paint has a significant impact on ROI. On average, for each gallon of paint you spend on the home you will see a return of $1000. If you spend 10 gallons of paint you will a property value increase of $10,000. There are small improvements that can be made to the home such as security upgrades/smart devices, but the bulk of your budget will be allocated on the big upgrades. We'll show you how to spend small on those big upgrades and which kitchen/bathroom updates provide the highest ROI (ones that you can upgrade on a budget). We focus upgrades based on market demand, and the following upgrades are the most sought-after on the US real-estate market.

Bearing that in mind, the following 4 upgrades will increase the value of your property significantly:

Renovation #1) The Kitchen

The phrase "The Kitchen is the heart of the home" holds true - you must start your renovations with the kitchen. The main cosmetic upgrades you must make are inside the kitchen - if the counters are too outdated you have to replace them or paint them. People will analyze the state of the kitchen first to get a sense for the state of the rest of the house. Families spend a lot of time in the kitchen and buyers have very specific demands as to the amenities they require. Most people don't wish to fiddle with small purchases and prefer everything delivered turnkey, which is why they'll expect you to present them with a fully remodeled kitchen. The kitchen has to have the newest appliances such as fridges, trendy stoves, double-sinks, kitchen islands, microwaves, dishwashers and more. The more "modern" your appliances the faster the property will sell. You want the average buyer to imagine themselves waking up and having coffee on that kitchen countertop. The kitchen can get very expensive as smart appliances alone could run up to thousands of dollars. Turkey kitchens are also more expensive than individually purchasing appliances. This is why we focus on small improvements that have a big impact on kitchen renovations.

- **Kitchen Upgrade #1:** Double Sink
- **Average Cost**: $100-$50

Replace the sink with a double-sink: This is a cheap, popular upgrade that is viewed as an essential by the majority of Millennial and younger generation buyers. Surveys show that middle-income buyers require a double-sink as a necessity and they need enough space to store all their large pots and pens. The deeper the sink, the more space they have, the better. Aim for a sink that is going to contain splashes and allow enough space to contain multiple large pots, pans and dishes. The sink doesn't have to be extravagant: It can be a simple, functional and easy to clean sink. Purchase a sink with a modern touch to add to the "premium" feeling of the kitchen.

- **Kitchen Upgrade #2**: Kitchen Island
- **Average Cost**: $200-500

The most sought-after feature in kitchens is a kitchen-island. Fortunately, kitchen islands are affordable upgrades and can be found for under $500. Almost 80% of all new home-buyers require a kitchen island as an essential, and the island is synonymous with American kitchen culture. Families require a space where they can carve their groceries, prepare coffee/smoothies, entertain guests, talk in the morning and store their essentials. The kitchen sink provides additional eating space to the main table (very desirable kitchen feature!) and it adds storage space separate from the main fridge. The kitchen will center around the kitchen island and you might want to allocate more of your budget on the island because it sets the tone of the kitchen. Most kitchen islands are "pre made" which means they can fit into all empty spaces.

- **Kitchen Upgrade #3**: Paint Cabinets
- **Average cost**: $30-50/gallon of paint

Does your property come with old kitchen cabinets? Replacement cabinets are affordable but what's more affordable is painting them! You can reshape the vibe of a kitchen by re-painting the rusty old cabinets with a simple brush in under 1 hour. If the room feels too "small" and "dark" this can be a result of old dark cabinets that need refreshing. The quickest cure for a dark room is to liven up the colors by opening it up with light colors. We recommend neutral white or grey paint that will create the illusion of space and brighten the room. These neutral colors are welcoming and paint only costs $30-50/gallon. The effects on the kitchen will be significant and you can save money instead of replacing the cabinets.

Renovation #2) The Bathroom

Flipping Houses

The bathroom provides ROI on a 2x average basis: If you invest $15,000 in a bathroom the buyer will think you invested $30,000. For example, you can install new three-light fixtures for under $100 that give the bathroom a five-star hotel look and the buyer will think you invested thousands in the light fixtures of the bathroom. A ready "turnkey" bathroom can cost tens of thousands of dollars. To get around that, you have to remodel the most important essentials of a bathroom such as shower stall, fixtures, toilets, vanity and shower heads. These upgrades are cheap and cost a few hundred dollars at most. If you combine the most essential upgrades, you can modernize the bathroom without overspending. Concentrate on the details: Purchase modern upgrades that give the bathroom a fresh start. The following are the most essential upgrades that increase the outlook of a bathroom significantly:

- **Bathroom Upgrade #1**: Fixtures (handles, faucets, and shower heads)
- **Average Cost**: $100-$200

The main cosmetic upgrades in the bathroom are the fixtures - if you replace fixtures with modern fixtures it gives the bathroom a shiny and clean feeling, almost as if you bought a turnkey bathroom. This boosts the appeal of the bathroom significantly. Star overhauling the bathroom by installing new shower-heads or faucets. If you have old rusty shower heads with visible tear and wear, this is very bad for the image of the bathroom. New shower-heads can be replaced for under $100. Dismantle the old flickering light at the ceiling and purchase new three-way light fixtures that are modern and illuminate the room in bright LED light. For the sink faucet, purchase one with a new brushed nickel finish that adds style. Purchase a nickel showerhead for efficient water usage and shininess. Consider a new light fixture above the vanity which will usually cost under $100.

- **Bathroom Upgrade #2**: Toilets
- **Average Cost**: $100-200 (+ $300 for installation).

The main upgrade new clients will appreciate in a bathroom is a new toilet! Most time in the bathroom is spent on the toilet and clients don't want to use toilets that were used by other people for years. You want to purchase and replace the toilet with a spanking new one. Many outdated toilets also have bowls that leak gallons of water at night without your knowledge which makes this an essential upgrade. Fortunately toilets can cost as low as $100 and the most expensive ones are below $300. Installation costs are higher than the toilet itself, but you can find deals in places like Home Depot which installs toilets for under $300. Many new toilets come with different color options and flush the water in a powerful way. If you want to upgrade the toilet consider adding a bidet which many clients will appreciate.

- **Bathroom Upgrade #3**: Vanity
- **Average Cost**: $200-$500

The vanity is a bathroom essential of similar significance to the toilet because the vanity is a part of our morning and night routines! The vanity is the first thing we use in the morning and the last thing we use at night. We place our essentials in the vanity and you want to make sure the vanity is something your new clients would want to use daily. The vanity can bring significant returns on the bathroom. Focus on the details to see if you can repaint or fix the current vanity before you purchase a new one. If you repaint the vanity use neutral colors such as white, grey or beige. A new vanity can cost up to $500 depending on the materials used and the size of the vanity. Your vanity must have a new modern countertop, a sink, faucet with decent height and a clean finish. If there is an outdated mirror you can replace it with a cheap one, expanding the space in the room and giving it a sleeker, modern look.

Renovation #3) Flooring/Carpeting

- **Average Cost**: $6-10/sq ft.

The floor in the living room is one of the "big 3" upgrades aside from kitchen and bathroom. If you upgrade the living room floor you can add significant value to the resell price of your property - everyone wants a new floor. The average cost of a new floor is $6-10 per square foot. This means that the floor of a large living room can be completely replaced for under $1000. However, it doesn't mean that you can't go lower. There are certain materials that can go for as little as $3/square foot. If you opt for the most luxurious materials you will pay up to $20/square foot. This depends on the total makeover and/or impression you're trying to create on buyers. The quality of the floor is one of the first things they'll notice aside from the paint-job. Floors are something you can't do on your own, however, labor costs are not exuberant and the average 300 sq. ft living room can be replaced for $1000 not including materials. The floor is a huge upgrade for a new house because the owners won't have to bother getting it replaced themselves. You can completely reshape the vibe of the living room: If you purchase black-colored floors, the home will have a more modern and neutral look. To complete the flooring upgrades purchase a modern carpet that your new buyers will love. As a rule of thumb, copy floors in your neighborhood.

Renovation #4) Install Patio/Deck

➢ **Average Cost**: $2000-4000/patio

The biggest value-booster in certain states is installing a patio or a deck. Does the home have a back yard where you can install an additional patio to lay down chairs and relax? Building one can boost the property value significantly. People who love to entertain in warmer states will find this a plus because they can enjoy an outdoor space to relax, cook, eat, drink, play with children and hold events. There is the possibility to extend the patio to the pool area if there is a pool in the back of the house.

The patio converts the house into a "summer oasis" where the owners can host parties and bring guests over. Patios are a great investment because they enable future owners to create long-lasting memories and many owners would pay more if they have a good patio. The installation cost is not exuberant: The average concrete patio costs $700 in materials, and once labor costs/contractors are added it amounts to $2000-4000 per patio. A small investment of this kind can re-shape the vibe of the property; however, in colder states this is not desirable as there's less time to enjoy the outdoors.

Curb Appeal: What It Is & How to Do It Right

Curb appeal is a term used to describe the first impression a person gets when they drive past a house. Drive past a row of house - what's the first thing you think about them? Do you think "That's a nice house" or "That house sucks" when you drive past them? Your reaction is determined by the curb appeal! If the house has a good curb appeal, you will have a good first impression. If the house has a bad curb appeal, you have a bad first impression. Curb appeal is determined by the exterior: the paint job of the house, the light fixtures, the lawn, patio, cars parked and other minor details. The curb appeal translates to pictures taken online as people open houses based on the state of the exterior - if they like the exterior they want to see the interior. In essence, your house could be falling apart on the inside but if the exterior looks maintained it will have a good curb appeal for passer-bys. To improve curb appeal, we focus on exterior decorations, re-painting, landscaping and general maintenance.

The HOA (Homeowners Association) focuses on curb appeal by hiring contractors who power-wash and maintain public driveways. This way each home in the neighborhood is maintained and the neighborhood can maintain high property values. If a resident of an HOA community refuses to pay they can be fined as they signed a legal document to own in a community with mandatory maintenance. Home-owners and building contractors use multiple ways to increase the curb appeal which makes the house more valuable. Buyers want to see a property in good shape before they sign a mortgage: They want to feel "at home". To create this, you must make upgrades that will create a homely feeling for the new buyers.

Curb appeal is also the reaction your neighbors have once they walk/drive past your house - it's not only appeal to buyers. Example: If you walk past a neighbors property and think "Wow his outdoor lighting enhances the landscaping" you reinforce the positive impressions you have of their home. Children playing can also be a sign of high curb appeal as children only play in front lawns that have lush green turf ideal for sport activities. Before you try to sell a property, you want to maximize the curb appeal it has because this will create good first impressions for future buyers. You want to assign a certain percentage of your renovation budget to essentials that increase curb appeal and make the house appealing to future buyers. Upgrades that boost curb appeal significantly are exterior paint and light fixtures: Curb-appeal essentials can be upgraded for a few thousand dollars and the increase in home value will be significant.

Curb Appeal Booster #1: Exterior Paint

➢ **Average Cost**: $100-200/2-3 gallons (+$20 for brushes!)

The paint job gives the impression that the home is maintained and in good shape. Cosmetic upgrades on the home increase home value significantly and the most essential of such is the exterior paint. Re-painting your home will attract buyers and increase the value of your property. New paint will not only renew the look of the property but it will keep it safe against the elements. For each gallon you put in the exterior paint-job, you will see a return of $1000/gallon.

Note: Painting the exterior is ideal for homes that are in decent shape and could use a renewal - it won't do much for a decaying property that requires new walls and insulation.

Contractors might increase the price of a paint job by a margin of 2-3x. The best way to save money on an exterior paint is to paint it yourself. Bring your dad or brother in law and paint the home yourselves - it should take you no longer than 2 days to paint a 2000 sq foot home exterior. If you're on a budget this is a huge money-saver. Focus on covering all the blemishes and camouflage any peeling spots. Make sure the color matches the exteriors of other homes in the area. On average, you will spend $30-50 per gallon of paint. This means that to cover the exterior you will need only $100-200 depending on the size of the house. Equipment such as brushes and supplies will add up to only $20-30. Then you're on to painting! The paint will boost your curb appeal and it should be done at the end of your renovations, to remain fresh for the realtor showings and "open houses" that sell the property.

Curb Appeal Booster #2: Smart LEDs

➢ **Average Cost**: $100-200

Exterior light can increase curb appeal and deter criminals - this is a win-win. Exterior light is one of the key essential features that new home buyers look for and newer "smart" lights are desirable as they illuminate the front entire patio/driveway and can be activated using motion sensors. New lights are energy-efficient and can light up the front of your house for the entire night without costing you a fortune. For under $300 in light fixtures, you can convert cold patios into warm and welcoming spaces that create an evening ambience for guests and showings.

The realtor can show your property at night and display a warm atmosphere that will sell the house. LED lights are very desirable as they build a cozy atmosphere and keep the home safe. Installation is prompt and new fixtures can be attached and installed in under an hour. To finalize your light upgrades, purchase motion-sensor activated headlights that you place above the garage. If you want to maximize your curb appeal at night, consider purchasing waterproof solar fairy LED's that you can lay out all along your front yard fence that will create a homely feeling for passerby's.

Small Updates for a Significantly More Desirable Home

Congratulations – you've made the big upgrades! Let's assume you've spent $5000 on a kitchen and $10,000 on a bathroom - each property has unique requirements based on the state of the interior. The property you buy might have had a bad bathroom with a new(ish) kitchen. In that case you assign 50% of your renovation budget on the bathroom and make small upgrades on the rest. The important factor is to "even out" the home with equal standards throughout each room. You don't want to have a smart kitchen and then a 60s decrepit bathroom in the next room. Congratulations – you've made the big upgrades! What happens once you've done all the big renovations and you're ready to sell on the market? There are numerous small upgrades that cost under $1000 which can help secure and "smartify" the home. Buyers will purchase a home branded as "smart" even if it's more expensive than a regular home in good shape. The surprising fact is that most security gadgets and smart features cost only a few hundred dollars. In theory, you could equip the home with the latest technology by spending almost no money.

We focus on 3 minor upgrades: security systems, smart tech and landscaping. Those upgrades provide the highest bang for your buck and ROI on homes. Statistically the US has a burglary every 18 seconds and it makes sense to equip your property with the latest security tech. Most "all in one" security systems come with cameras, motion sensors and Smartphone app compatibility. We also recommend installing smart thermostats that help buyers configure the temperature in their home. Finally we recommend minor landscaping upgrades that can increase the curb appeal of the home. The following minor upgrades will significantly impact the value of your property:

Value Upgrade #1) Wireless Security Systems

➢ **Average Cost**: $50-$200

Security systems operate wirelessly via WiFi and can be installed in under an hour: Most home-security packages you purchase on Amazon can provide you with multiple security cameras to cover every angle and interior of the house. You can install a camera on the front of the house, the living room, the back porch and any areas you desire. The camera's motion sensors will pick up on movement and send you signals to your smartphone while you're at work using WiFi. Advanced camera systems can also identify smoke and prevent house fires. If you spend a few more bucks, you can purchase a camera that has night vision to protect you from burglars at night (or even help capture criminals if your neighbor's home is burglarized by monitoring the immediate neighborhood!). Many security cameras have backup batteries that help them operate while you're on vacation or in case of a power outage.

The average smart security camera costs $50-100, but a full set can be had in the $200-300 range that includes multiple cameras for 24/7 security. Make sure the camera you purchase is DYI (do it yourself) and allows you to install the system on your own. To save money, purchase security systems that don't have monthly subscription systems. Many manufacturers hook clients on monthly fees to use their security software - find ones that come without monthly charges. Security systems will enhance the safety of the home and help sell it easier.

Value Upgrade #2) Smart Thermostat

➢ **Average Cost**: $200-400

Research shows that one of the cheapest and fastest ways to smartification and increasing property value is to install a high-tech thermostat. The benefits of smart thermostats are numerous: They save time, conserve energy, adapt to your lifestyle and help you configure the temperate of your home. The best all-around thermostats you can find on Amazon will analyze the work patterns of the residents and use that to lower the heat when they're at work and turn it up once they're back home. Thermostats take under an hour to install and can be done DYI: They have low maintenance and work in conjunction with smartphone apps. The best systems cost in the range of $200-400, depending on the coverage. This feature will sell a home fast and it can be one of the main talking points once you show it off to buyers.

Value Upgrade #3) Landscaping

➢ **Average Cost**: $50-$100

Lawns increase property value and many HOA communities enforce laws for lawn maintenance, fining residents who fail to adhere to the guidelines. The lawn has to be green and well-maintained with no yellow patches or ground holes. Research shows that in house-flipping adequate maintenance of the lawn recovers 100% of the initial renovation costs at the time of the sale and can boost the home value by 5-10%. To maintain a lawn you can hire a contractor or do it yourself (best money saver!). Go to the hardware store and purchase hedge trimmers and a lawn mower that you can use to start working.

If you want to upgrade your lawn, plant primrose bushes or use pavers to line the driveway. This will boost the curb appeal of your home significantly, and primrose bushes are very easy to maintain. If you have any yellow spots you can get paint and fill them in before you start taking pictures or showing them to buyers. These changes take a few hours of work at most and they have a serious impact on the perception and value of your property.

Value Upgrade #4) New Ceiling Fans

➢ **Average Cost**: $100/fan + $100 for installation

Real estate institute research shows that ceiling fans are loved by buyers of all income brackets - if the home lacks ceiling fans you can add them for less than $100 each. The ceiling fan adds extra lighting and comfort. If your property is in a warm state, you absolutely need ceiling fans. There should be a ceiling fan in the living room and each bedroom: That will create a homely feeling as you navigate the house. If you're unsure as to whether ceiling fans are practical in your area, analyze the comps or visit properties nearby and consult with the residents. The ceiling fan design has to be minimalistic and not "overwhelm" the room you're renovating. The go-to ceiling fan design is pure matte black with wooden blades.

Green Improvements that Instantly Increase a Home's Value

Energy efficiency is a term for upgrading the house with equipment that preserves heat or keep the home cool, saving on costs. Energy efficiency does not have to be expensive! Yes, a solar panel installation will cost $14,000 on average but mere upgrades such as replacing the windows can cost only $2000-3000 a house. Energy-efficiency multiplies each dollar you put in the property by a multiplier of 2x. If you invest $5000 in energy-efficiency you will get $10,000 back. If you update the energy-efficiency of a house you can convince your future buyers that they're buying an energy-efficient house using hard numbers. In states like California all new developments have to have solar panels or they are not eligible for a building permit. If you want to upgrade the home for complete energy efficiency without relying on the public grid, you can do this for as little as $15,000. The price will depend upon the quality of the panels and the size of the home. Similar rules apply for making small upgrades such as the insulation or window replacement.

Simple upgrades can make the home green and boost energy-efficiency. **Example**: Replacing age-old windows with new double-paned windows can reduce cooling bills by 15% and save the residents $500 a year in utility costs. LED lights are ultra-conservative on energy and the electricity is virtually for free once you switch to LED fixtures. If you replace each light in the house with a new LED fixture, you can explain how the lighting system of the house is built for longevity and how they'll save on electricity bills in the long run. Seek out government-funded energy efficiency initiatives in your state, as many states will subsidize the purchases of energy-efficient windows, lights and solar panels. The following are the most popular upgrades that you can install on virtually every home in the US:

Green Upgrade #1) Energy-Efficient Windows

Average Cost: $150-300/window

Windows have impact on heat penetration that comes in and leaves the property - almost as much as insulation. If the insulation of the property is on par with modern standards, the windows have to be brought up to par to withstand every climate. The weather is getting more extreme in both the summer and the winter: The summers are hotter and the winters are colder. The newest windows that have an "Energy Star" rating are desirable and considered environmentally-friendly. Windows will boost the property value by a multiplier of 2x similar to solar panels. Vinyl windows are the go-to for flippers because they are easy to install/maintain, durable, energy-efficient and environmentally friendly. The average price per window is $150-300 depending on the size of the window. If the home has 20 windows, you can replace each window in the house for as low as $3000.

Green Upgrade #2) Solar Panels

Average Cost: $10,000-15,000/house

Solar panels are the ultimate upgrade in green energy - certain states are now mandating that to get a building permit each new construction has to have solar panels. They're a go-to upgrade for all warm states because the year-round sunshine can provide easy energy-efficiency and the investment pays off in as little as 10 years. Solar panels help harvest the energy of the natural environment. To equip a house for 100% energy-efficiency using solar panels, you will spend on average $10,000-15,000 for the whole house. The total costs may exceed $20,000 in some states but every state subsidizes solar panels which brings down the average significantly. There are many tax rebates and credits you can apply on the federal and state levels once you switch to solar panels. This will be considered a major upgrade for all homes and make it an easy sell because the new buyer doesn't have to haggle installing them. The average solar system with 20 solar panels will only take 1-3 days to install. This is an easy upgrade if you have the budget and you deem it necessary in your state.

Each dollar that you invest in energy-efficiency will provide a magnificent return once it's time to sell! The only downside is that this is not a priority for low-cost flips. It's also not practical for cold states. Analyze how much energy the property you're purchasing consumes currently and how much it will save after the energy-efficient upgrades are made. There are upgrades for every budget and for maximum energy-efficiency the average person won't have to exceed $20,000 - that includes all solar panel installations, LED upgrades, insulation and window upgrades.

Chapter 6 - Making It Shine

Putting Together the Rehab Dream Team

You've financed the deals, you signed the checks, you bought your first house! Congratulations! The next step is to assemble your "Dream Team" of contractors, lawyers and real-estate professionals. Who would ever need a lawyer, you might ask? Every financial transaction you make will have to be documented by lawyers who can ensure you don't end up with lawsuits and your accountant/CPA will take care of your taxes to keep you safe from Uncle Sam. Contractors can make our break your deal, and assembling a team of contractors is essential - there are many ways to save money on contractors which we'll distill below.

In real estate you can hire "General Contractors/GC's" who do all the rehab work at once (re-structuring, painting, flooring, roofing) or you can hire sub-contractors for each one of those individual professions. It's easy to find each one of those professionals - they're all connected and working together. Once you have a friend who is in real estate, you can get referrals to contractors in your area. There is also the possibility to look them up online, as many contractors operate in their immediate area exclusively. It's very rare to meet a construction crew in California that came all the way from Florida. Flipping is done the old-fashioned way on a community basis.

Your "Dream Team" has to be assembled based on an essential and non-essential basis. Some people are absolutely essential: Lawyers and contractors. Other people are not essential: Realtors and architects. The rules change: Contractors can be non-essential if you're familiar with construction work and can carry out repairs yourself. However, for most flippers trade work is out of the equation because it requires a lot of expertise and it's risky to do jobs you're not familiar with (for safety and legal reasons). Don't make mistakes and end up with a lawsuit at start of your flip - hire an attorney to look at each end of the sale, the purchase documents and the closing sale. There's a reason some lawyers charge $500/hour - once they've overlooked the details to your sale in that single hour, they can estimate mistakes that might cost you thousands of dollars in long-term costs or a potential lawsuit.

Remember: You hire professionals at every stage of the flip. Your "Dream Team" won't work with you for the duration of the whole flip. At the start you will need to mobilize a lawyer to look over your avulsion and financing papers. Once you've had a lawyer's seal of approval, you can proceed with the purchase. You will then need to decide if you want to hire a 'General Contractor' who will carry out all repairs for you at a negotiated cost, or hire sub-contractors for the individual branch of work you need done. We'll teach you how to pick out the best contractors for the lowest price. If this is your first project, you're best off hiring a GC in your area who will carry out all repairs for once. Accountants are necessary after each flip to analyze the financial documents and estimate your taxes before and after. Landscapers and handymen might be needed depending on the state of your property. Architects are only necessary if you plan to tear down or add space which requires special drawings and permits. Finally, realtors can help you sell a home and do all the work for you for a commission. The following 2 categories highlight which people you will need to hire to get started in house-flipping:

Essential Professionals

1) Lawyers.

The lawyer is the most essential piece of the puzzle: They draw up the contractors before you purchase a property and settle the sale once you've sold a property. They can identify flaws in your contracts that you never knew existed and/or could lead to lawsuits. To be safe, always pick a lawyer who specializes in real estate rather than general practice. Real estate lawyers in your area will be familiar with local zoning laws and they're especially useful if you plan to add or remove space to get permits for construction. Lawyers will inform you if your flipping practices are compliant with local laws. Lawyers charge high hourly rates because their job demands a lot of attention to detail and they'll have to review the deal first, in addition to being present at inspections and closings. Many lawyers starting out will agree to work with as little as $100-150 an hour because they're trying to make a name for themselves. The average for an established real estate lawyer can be $200-300/h and you only need them for a few hours each month. Some lawyers will agree to work for a $1000-2000 advance payment on each flip no matter how many hours they work.

> **Average Cost**: $150-300/h

2) Accountants.

Accountants/CPAs are an essential piece of the puzzle that work alongside lawyers. The accountant or "CPA" is in charge of all your financial details and keeps track of the taxes you must pay and advise you on tax rebates that you can write off. If you hire a CPA you will find out which items you've invested in can be "written off" on your tax records. For example, if you purchase solar panels a CPA can tell you how much you can write off for that purchase in your state and save you money. They can help you establish your business structure file all your taxes for you and ensure your financial documents are in order for flippers who do multiple flips per year. Most CPAs will require 1 or 2 hours a month to handle your documents and offer "monthly plans" or you can pay a yearly $1000-2000 to a CPA to have them on call and file your documents on April 15th.

> **Average Cost**: $500-1000/year

3) General Contractors/GCs.

The most essential piece of the puzzle once your legal documents are settled are the people who actually make renovations happen! General Contractors or "GC's" in short can oversee your entire rehabilitation effort and a single person hires their own qualified professionals who can repair a property swiftly without involving multiple crews. General Contractors specialize in all trades at once and their crews are experienced with all renovation types. They can renovate the kitchen, bathroom, floors, tear down/add space, or anything required to complete your renovation. This decreases the potential for error as a single crew is in charge of the renovations and you don't have to deal with a set of sub-contractors, one of which might turn out unreliable. Once you've found a General Contractor you only have to worry about the sale of the property because they will carry out all renovations without you lifting a finger. General Contractors don't charge hourly fees but they settle on a fixed renovation cost based on your budget and their estimated costs: They will give you a bid and if you agree on the bid they will carry out all renovations within that budget range.

➢ **Average Cost**: Negotiated

Non-Essential Professionals

1) Realtors.

Most houses in the US are sold through realtors: These are licensed professionals who specialize in the sales process of a house. They handle all the listing/marketing, presentations, showings and they ensure a final sale on the property. Realtors charge significant commissions for their work and some realtors can take 6% on the sale of a house (3% for the buyer's realtor and 3% for the seller's realtor). However, their knowledge as to the market data for neighborhoods, sales tactics and sweat equity compensate for their commissions (which are negotiable). Realtors are paid by sellers/flippers and if you choose to hire a realtor you will have to pay them out of pocket based on a pre-agreed fee. Realtors are useful for people trying to fix multiple properties who don't have time to deal with buyers first-hand.

➢ **Average Cost**: 6%/sale

2) Landscapers.

Landscapers boost the curb appeal of the property and make the exterior look more appealing to buyers. Landscapers are usually hired on an "as-needed" basis as they're only necessary once the final repairs are carried out and you need to put the finishing touches on a property. Basic landscaping such as lawn mowing is something you can do on your own, but landscapers can help re-grow dead grass or cover up yellow patches. They can also position plants, trim your existing garden and ensure everything is adequate and ready to sell. The average landscaper will work for $60/h not including materials.

➤ **Average Cost**: $50-70/h

3) Architects.

Architects are non-essential in "house-flipping" because architects design the new – you're buying and selling existing properties. Architects specialize in drawing up and estimating structural size to ensure the building will be structurally-sound and their work is required before a construction crew goes to work. However, once the house is built architects are only required once you need to remove a room/change the structure or add more space on the exterior. Architects are also hired on an "as-needed" basis and they can be quite costly with an average of $100/h. Many architects will agree to work for a fixed fee and are open to negotiations.

➤ **Average Cost**: $70-150/h

4) Handymen.

Handymen are general workers who give you a hand (as the name implies) and technically a handyman could be your father, brother in law, wife, or the student who lives down the street and need a few extra dollars. Handymen will be essential because many times you need someone to help you paint the rooms, patch up holes, install new cabinets and change the interior of the home. A handyman doesn't need to be licensed as they'll mostly be assisting with regular work. Handymen can be hired on the internet and many have extensive experience in construction and can help you with all your needs. The average you should pay a handyman is $30-60/h and try to get as much done in those hours to get the most bang for your buck.

➤ **Average Cost**: $30-60/h

5) Assistants.

Once you've made it big in flipping and you're starting to make 5-10 flips a year, hire a personal assistant who can be present on location with you and help you with your daily activities. This must be someone you can trust and it's recommended to hire inside your family to not get tricked. An assistant is a person who will be with you at the job site, dealing with contractors, meeting financiers, closing deals and delivering your papers to lawyers. An assistant can take 50% of the work load off your back. This is why it's better to hire inside the family – if their livelihood depends on the job, they'll be much more motivated.

> **Average Cost**: Negotiated

How do you find the general contractors, lawyers and individual sub-contractors? The answer: Classified ads in your local area. In most cases you can pop-over at a construction site and ask the workers to see the "boss" and have a chat with them: They will give you referrals for general contractors in your city. Make sure that the contractors you hire are licensed and experienced - they must have the know-how to carry out the professional tasks you hire them to. This will save you money because you won't have to pay for the same job twice.

How to Find the Best Contractor for Your Property

House-flipping is a team effort and all experienced house-flippers hire contractors at a certain point. There are no rules written in stone: One could purchase a house, renovate it themselves, and sell the house on their own - bypassing all contractor and realtor fees. However, in practice it's better to hire professionals who will carry out a high-quality job and allow you the time to focus on multiple projects at once. Hiring contractors is the hardest piece of the puzzle as you'll have to do almost as much research as you did buying a house. The contractors will oversee all your rehabilitations and renovations and a General Contractor can provide the material, labor, equipment/tools and render all those services at once.

General Contractors Vs Sub-Contractors

Flipping Houses

House-flipping schools of thought differ on the whole "debate" of GC's vs sub-contractors. GC's are known to get things done at once, but sub-contractors are deemed economical as they're only hired on an "as needed" basis. A good GC can carry out all renovations at a fixed price without over-charging you for unexpected surprises. General contractors are better for flippers who want to take a more "hands off" approach and focus on financing multiple projects at once. They save time and allow a flipper to focus on securing more finances, finding buyers and locating new properties. However, sub-contractors are better if you know your property only requires one or two repairs and you can hire sub-contractors for those repairs specifically.

GC's are have "crews" that can dispatch to your location and rehabilitate the property in a single swing. The boss will have a crew of guys who he manages under his wing and they will assign work based on the needs of your property. The benefit for flippers is that you're only paying one contractor for the whole renovation. This way you don't have to seek out and hire individual sub-contractors every time you need a room painted, a bathroom sink installed or a floor changed - the GC takes care of all that for you! General Contractors can be quite large and many of them work on multiple properties at once, managing hundreds of workers. They can switch employees between job sites. If one carpenter finishes a job at a certain property and your property requires a carpenter, they can be dispatched to your location.

To finalize the debate, ask yourself the following question: "Are my changes cosmetic?". If the changes you need on your property are cosmetic, you don't need a GC. If the renovations are focused on kitchen improvements (replacing sinks, appliances, countertops, kitchen islands, etc), bathroom renovations (toilets, counters, mirrors, sinks), paint-jobs (interior and exterior), floor changes (new floors) and landscaping - you can make these 'cosmetic' upgrades on your own or with the help of a few sub-contractors. If the renovations are larger and they require work on the foundation of the property and/or adding space you should hire a General Contractor.

General Contractors can work with architects and they can carry out demolitions/add-ons depending on what you need - they will help you get the drawings in order and get the building permits you need from your municipality before you build. Significant changes such as adding square footage, tearing down walls, adding rooms, changing roofs, foundation changes, etc, - those will all require General Contractors.

How To Discover Contractors

The real estate industry is "old fashioned" and most connections in the business are made through real-life interaction with contractors and referrals. You'll have to attend conferences, shake hands, call people and/or visit construction sites.

➢ **Referrals**. Join your local real estate investment group or attend conferences where you can meet people. A referral can be given by virtually any person: Fellow entrepreneur, flipping competitors, or even your neighbor. Ask real estate investors in the area who they've worked with and who they can vouch for. In many cases, you'll hear the same few names as usually big firms dominate a certain area. Inquire as to the efficiency and budgeting of the contractor (especially when hiring a GC). Ask if they finished the projects on time as delays can cost you thousands of dollars and ask about the total budget. If possible, visit properties that the GCs have worked on in the past.

➢ **Visit construction sites**. If you spot a construction site on your daily commute, park your car and talk to the workers there or talk to the boss if he's present on the job site. Flag down a worker and make a simple introduction. Say that you're going to need repairs and ask them how you can get in touch with their company for potential work. They will likely put you in touch with their boss and hand you a card - therefore allowing you to research them online and analyzing their past work.

➢ **Visit "building departments"**. Each city has a local "building department" that keeps track of which firms were granted construction permits - this way you can analyze firms that are operational at the moment and currently engaged with projects. It's possible that a firm went out of business if they were granted permits 3 years ago and you need recent data from the last 3-6 months. All General Contractors have to file for permits to do certain kind of work (mostly adding/removing rooms) and those have to pass inspections by city agents. If a contractor was granted a permit, that means they're doing top-notch work that complies with local building codes. The building department can provide you with information for all contractors currently operational in your area.

➢ **Online research**. Start with Google and look up "General Contractor + [Your City]" top find a list of General Contractors operational in your area. It's not recommend to opt for the first listings because they are the most popular and will charge the highest fees. Seek out lesser-known contractors that have a good reputation. An excellent source for local contractors and sub-contractors is Craigslist - advertising there is free and it's easy to discover many working contractors. Join real estate forums where flippers share insider information and can help you with any problem you stumble across.

Hire Licensed Contractors

Only hire licensed and insured contactors – GC's are not handymen that you can hire on the go. Your contractor has to be licensed in order to operate in your state and they must have insurance in case something goes wrong on your property (so you don't pay out of pocket!). A contractor should help you come up with a price sheet that will include prices by the sq. ft for things such as paint, floors, carpets. The sheet should include items that need replacing such as windows, fixtures, blinds, doors, appliances and more. Essential items have to be "pre agreed" therefore the contractor doesn't hit you by surprise with extra charges. Many times you won't work with the same contractors for longer than 6 months or a year - contractors come and go. Inform your contractors as to the exact amount you can afford to make sure their work is within the scope of your budget.

Pro Tip: You only negotiate with your contractor the first flip. Take your time to agree on the lowest price possible. If the contractor is successful, the next jobs won't require negotiations as you've already agreed on pre-set prices.

How To Pay Contractors

There are two ways to pay contractors: By-weekly or based on the work they've completed. Certain jobs might take longer than you initially planned for, and you should only pay based on the results. Refuse to pay contractors in advance because they might take your money and not complete the job. Make sure to compensate your contractors for each milestone completed. If they've finished the kitchen - pay them for the kitchen. If the renovate the whole house - pay them for the whole house. Never pay in advance for work that hasn't been completed.

Make It Shine While Minimizing Costs

You're ready to call contractors and negotiate prices: How do you sniff out which ones are going to do the most kick-ass job at the lowest price? How do you know if a contractor will over-charge you or give you a fair deal? In many cases there is nothing you can do about a bad contractor once you've agreed on a price - this is why you must cross-reference multiple contractors in advance. There are many methods you can employ to save money in advance such as investing in power-tools that you won't have to rent out for the job. If you have the tools necessary, you can watch tutorials and try to carry out the job yourself. Even if you hire contractors, they'll appreciate having an extra set of tools by their side. Aside from investing in power tools (important for all renovations!) you can hire dumpsters for the waste that will accumulate on the property and avoid the surcharges of a contractor bringing one. The following are the best ways to make your property shine without spending a lot of money:

Golden Rule #1) Call 3 Contractors At Once

You're new to the business - if you hire the GC you come across there's a 50% chance you'll make a profit and 50% chance they'll overcharge you and send your investment in a downward spiral. How do you decide which contractor to go for? Make them enter a bid war! Gather a list of the most appropriate contractors in your area based on their rate and call them each individually. Describe your property and needs to the contractor and once they have your details ask the magical question: "What is your bid?". The contractor will give you an approximate estimate based on the materials needed, the extent of the job and the time necessary. They may even reveal certain details about the job that you didn't realize were necessary. Most contractors bid by the square foot. For example, a flooring contractor will tell you how much the floor costs per square foot and the labor for each square foot assembled. Once you have 3 separate bids, you can make your decision based on which one is the lowest or best for the job. Calls are a real eye-opener because you can sense how truthful and knowledgeable the contractor is about the job! The more personal your interaction, the more you'll be aware of what to expect from that contractor.

Golden Rule #2) Ask About Fee Structure

If you have a general idea for the costs, you have to inquire as to the potential fee structure to understand if the contractor is familiar with house-flipping and the repeat business you can provide them. When you get in touch with a contractor ask them how much they would charge to complete a job for a 1500 sq. foot house. Let's say you need a full paint-job for the house that includes the ceilings. A "good" price for a paint-job of that kind would be $1/sq. foot or around $1500 total for the job. The contractor will quote you based on the size of the house and if they quote double ($3000) you know they aren't the right contractor for you. Which is good news! Because it means you're ready to move on to a more eligible contractor who knows the value of repeat business. Always inquire in terms of square footage: If you haven't bought a house yet, make up a random number such as 1500 square feet or 2000 square feet.

Money Saver #1) Free Planning

Flipping Houses

The best part about large department stores where you purchase merchandise is that many times they provide "free planning". This will save you copious amounts of money on interior designers once you're ready to renovate the big 3: The bathroom, bedrooms and living room. Most home-improvement stores you drive past will have designers on hand who will help you draft up a free plan if you purchase your materials from the store. Make sure the store you're buying from has a free "design consultation". In essence, you're getting a free interior designer who will re-design the shape of your interior at no charge.

Money Saver #2) Buying Overstocked Materials

Visit the local building-supply store or a large hardware store that supplies a huge chunk of the hardware market in your area. Those stores usually have "overstocked" merchandise that is sitting around in their back isles. Once you're at the store ask to talk to the manger and then inquire as to items you need that are in their inventory. It's possible to purchase overstocked items at discounts of up to 50% if you only engage with the manager. This is essential once you're buying power tools for your first flip.

Money Saver #3) Purchase Power Tools

You only have to do this once! The average power-tool costs between $50-100 and you can purchase a full set of power tools that you can use on your jobs for as little as $1000 - you will be using these power tools for years. When you pay a contractor, you're paying for their tools indirectly. If you rent tools, you have to return them and you can't re-use them on future jobs. Once you buy your own tools, they're there forever! If you prefer to save on your renovations and you're a DYI type, the following are the most essential tools you'll need for flipping job:

- **Power Washer** (to clean the decks/siding/exterior): $100-200.
- **Power Roller** (for painting interiors): $50-100.
- **Cordless Drill** (for drilling work): $50-100.
- **Screw Gun** (for "hard to do" screwing): $30-100.
- **Circular Saw** (for all wood cutting): $50-200.

- **Nail Gun** (for nail driving): $150-400.
- **Heat Gun** (for striping paint and wallpapers): $100-200.
- **Sanders** (for sanding scratches on wood): $100-200.
- **Reciprocating Saw** (if the circular saw is not enough): $50-150.

Money Saver #4) Hire Students

Young people are willing to work for a lot less than an established contractor - in many cases young people will agree to work a full day for a payment of $50. You can hire students looking for work to do basic jobs such as weeding, cleaning, vacuuming or window washing.

Money Saver 5) Rent A Dumpster

Renovating is a "messy" job - you'll be left with a mountain of garbage once you're done and you must dispose of that. General Contractors apply extra charges for dumpsters which they rent and transport to a landfill. Many companies rent out dumpsters where the workers can dispose of garbage on a monthly fee. If you use the same dumpster rental company they can give you discounts being a loyal customer.

Chapter 7 - Completing the Flip

The Lowdown on Selling Your Property Yourself vs. Through a Realtor

You've made it - your $50,000 house is now worth $100,000! The money you invested in the house is now all reflected in the glitzy kitchen, the suburb bathrooms and updated interior. You've completed each step of the renovation and you're ready to sell the house and collect your paycheck. Should you give the average 6% commission (the equivalent of $6000) to realtors? Should you make a "for sale by owner" listing to save yourself to save that 6% on the realtor commissions? Decision, decision, decision!

What are the best ways to save money and sell a house? There are 2 main ways to sell a house: 1) Through a realtor and 2) On your own (for sale by owner - "FSBO"). If you choose a realtor you're giving them permission to take over the entire selling process: The staging, marketing and selling. You're also giving the realtor a cut at the end of the sale which is determined by a fixed percentage as high as 6% of the total sale price. Realtors are hired for more expensive homes on average. In 2008 a study conducted by the National Association of Realtors determined that the median price of a home sold by a realtor was $211,000 while the median of for-sale-by-owner listing was $153,000. Does this mean owners can't sell houses without a realtor? Definitely not! There are numerous ways to sell a house on your own and save thousands of dollars on a realtor. However, hiring a realtor carries numerous benefits in terms of efficiency and time – it's almost like hiring your own personal assistant.

The following are benefits of hiring a realtor that you never knew existed:

Realtor Advantage #1) Buyer's Realtors Won't Show FSBO Listings

Flipping Houses

Realtors who help buyers buy houses might refuse to show FSBO (for sale by owner) listings. This is because they know there's not going to be another realtor who can meet them and help them with the other end of the transaction. The buyer's agent might refuse to show your home to a buyer even if the buyer is trying to make them go for a visit.

The realtor will cite that dealing with FSBO listings is dangerous to their clients and that they shouldn't purchase houses without a representative for the seller. They want to get a guaranteed commission and they're weary of listings that don't have realtors shaking their hand on the other end. If you choose to sell the house on your own, you must be aware that other realtors will be put off by your house and know how to market to buyers directly.

Realtor Advantage #2) Realtors Are Emotionally-Detached

Selling the home can be an emotionally-draining because you've put months of work into the property - you will be tempted to get rid of the property at the first decent bid offer. Realtors know how to negotiate to get your the highest price for each house. When you hire a realtor, you're removed from the everyday emotional aspect of dealing with clients first-hand and this makes you less prone to making stupid decisions. "Stupid" decisions include overpricing the home, not countering low offers because you're offended by a low offer, or expediting the decision-making if you set deadlines for the selling. A realtor won't have the sense of desperation a flipper who's invested 6 months in the property will. If you sell the property you will likely nervously check your phone for signals (messages from buyers, inquiries, etc) and this can your judgment and affect your decision-making. Remove yourself from the process.

Rejection is a big negative too - if a realtor brings a client over and you show them the home, but they later decide they don't want to purchase the home the realtor will have to take that rejection. The realtor will only inform you once the property is sold and they won't tell you about individual meetings when they were rejected. It might be upsetting to hear some of the comments of potential buyers if you renovated the home yourself and this is why a neutral person such as a realtor can assist by keeping a cool head when showing the property to prospects.

Realtor Advantage #3) Selling Requires 24/7 Meetings

Selling house is a full-time job. Realtors work around the clock to show each individual property depending on when the buyers are available. What if someone calls you to see the home and you're stuck at work? You miss a potential lead. What if you're at a meeting and you get a buyer calling you with questions about the house? You can't be bothered with it. If you're working the whole day (especially on multiple properties), do you have the energy to explain to buyers each individual aspect of a home time and time again? Do you have marketing skills to show off each individual feature of the home? This is what a realtor does - they work around the clock selling properties and meeting clients individually. Your job is to purchase properties, renovate them and get paid. Realtors are invaluable when you're tied up between multiple properties and you don't have time to sell each individual property.

Realtors will give clients such as yourself a lockbox for the front door that allows them to show the home to buyers when you're away. Once all renovations have commenced, you'll no longer have a reason to stick around the property and the realtor can take over the sales procedure.

Realtor Disadvantage #1) Realtors Take A Big Cut

The only downside to hiring realtors is their commission. Should you hire a realtor? It depends on your priorities: If you want to save money above all, a 6% commission would sit better in your pocket. If you're financing multiple flips and don't have time to fiddle with each potential buyer, you should hire a realtor to take the weight off your back. We recommend selling yourself on the first flip because you'll keep more money and you'll learn the ins and outs of selling houses. If you hire a realtor right off the bat, you'll miss out on interacting with buyers and the lessons that ensue. The main reason to hire a realtor is to save yourself time: They do all the selling, prep work and dealing with prospects for you. If you're in the middle of 5 properties, you want a realtor to take over the sales process for you and allow you to focus on renovating properties. The opposite holds true: If you're new to the business, you can save thousands of dollars by NOT hiring a realtor.

Pro Tip: Be patient. If you've made successful renovations and priced the home appropriately, the offers will come in. You might not like certain offers and you may have to wait for weeks after you've started advertising the home to get a proper offer. Remain patient and price your home realistically, and you will likely get a fast sale (under a month!).

5 Best Marketing Strategies for Real Estate

You're ready to list the house and start getting offers. It's time to market your property aggressively - if you've chosen to forgo a realtor you'll be competing with hundreds of realtors in your area. You must schedule the placement of your house on the most popular real estate websites, upload the photos, communicate with buyers, schedule showings, and close the sale yourself. These are all things your realtor will do once you hire them, but you can join the process and contribute your own to make the sale go smoother. Marketing strategies can be applied even if you hire a realtor as they will essentially use the same marketing strategies - the only difference is that the property is more "prestige" if it's sold through a realtor and realtors meet buyers in person. There are many things you can do before you apply marketing such as hire photographers, write good descriptions, price the home adequately and filter the buyers.

Prep Step #1) Take Professional Photos

First impression matters not only for curb appeal when buyers arrive for a showing but online when they're browsing through hundreds of listings. You want your listing to stand out! To make that happen, you need to have professionals to take professional photos. Your iPhone photoshoot might get the job done, but a professional photographer will have a wide range of lenses and equipment that can enhance the colors of the property and make it look even better than it does in real life. Most photographers also have drones which can take aerial photos to showcase the surrounding neighborhood if it's in a great area. Aerial photos can expedite the sell a property by a margin of 30%. Most photographers are cheap and won't charge you more than a few hundred dollars for the shoot and post-processing. For the impact they can have on the sale of a property, professional photography a must-have.

Prep Step #2) Write Creative Descriptions

The first thing people notice once they open your listing is the description – they want to see if it captivates their attention. You don't just want to write "2 bedroom 2 bath going for $200,000". You want to write "2 bed 2 bath dream home, 5 minutes away from [City Attraction] going for only $200,000!". Take a look at dozens of properties and notice which descriptions stand out. Copy the writing style of those descriptions and replace them with your own information. If the ad captivated your attention, it will have the same effect on another prospect. Make sure to double-check for spelling mistakes and proofread your listings before you publish them.

Prep Step #3) Set Smart Prices

House pricing on the internet does not work the same as on real-life appraisals. When you meet an appraiser and/or compile your list of "comps" you will get a general value appraisal - this doesn't mean you should use that appraisal as the sale price of the home. What sells a home on the internet is "smart pricing". Instead of listing the home for $200,000 it's much more effective to list it for $199,999. What impact will this have on the sale? On many websites people will narrow their search down based on price. If they search up to $200,000, they will be unable to see your listing. Smart pricing helps create a feeling of "affordability" because the property seems more affordable to the average person than the full price.

Prep Step #4) Filter Buyers

The main problem of online real estate websites is that they're open to all kinds of buyers: You might get interest from buyers who are not financially capable of purchasing a property. This is why realtors filter buyers in advance: The buyer's realtor checks their finances to make sure they're "qualified" and then they sends qualified leads to the seller's realtor based on the price range to make a quick sale. They in return get 3% each off the sale. The internet is the "wild west" in terms of prospects because you never know if they really mean business or they're wasting your time. Hiring a realtor who has connections to other realtors can help you save time by sending only qualified buyers at your location.

Top 5 Marketing Strategies For Real Estate

If you've successfully completed the creative work (photography, copywriting, pricing), it's time to make your property visible to future prospects. Even if your property is in top shape, you have the best pictures/aerial shots, you have good sales copy and pricing - no one will know your property exists unless you list it on big online websites. The following are the best ways to market a property on the internet (which are all free!):

Marketing Strategy #1) List On Real Estate Websites

To list your property online, start with the largest websites – the most prominent of which is Zillow. Zillow currently lists over 100 million properties for sale in the United States that include regular houses, condos, commercial buildings, foreclosures and more. Zillow can estimate the price of a property using similar listings and they have data for every zip code in the US. Their database is massive and they receive dozens of millions of visitors every day. A listing on Zillow will expose your property to thousands of potential buyers in your immediate area. The Zillow Group also owns Trulia.com which is a major player in the real estate industry. Currently listings on Zillow are free and they allow you to upload pictures, videos and key information about the property. Buyers will have access to your contact information and the ability to call/email you to pitch offers.

Marketing Strategy #2) List On Classified Ads Websites

The biggest classified websites on the internet are Craigslist and Nextdoor: Both of these are highly trafficked websites by people looking to purchase homes. Craigslist in particular is the largest classified ads website in the world and their listings are free, and you can re-create listings once your old listings expire. Craigslist will give you exposure to people in your area looking to purchase property and can make for a quick sale.

Marketing Strategy #3) Old-School Print Ads

Market the old-fashioned way - print out ads and plaster them in the immediate neighborhood. The people most interested in property in your area are going to be people who already reside there! Many times people are on the lookout for second investment homes that they can purchase and/or pass on to their children. If they're located right where they live, it's more convenient for them because they'll be able to stay in touch with family. You can print out a picture of your house, list basic details/sales price and plaster it all over the neighborhood such as local parks, bus stations, electric stands and more. You'll see ads like that all the time because this marketing strategy is still effective. If you want to take this a step further, hire a designer to make a brochure with your property that highlights the details of each room, and host "Open Days". Your realtor can help you organize open days that will last from the morning to the afternoon, typically on weekends. This leaves the home open for everyone who wants to check it out in person.

Marketing Strategy #4) Make A YouTube Video

You don't have to be Scorsese to make a "House Tour" for YouTube. To make a YouTube video, all you have to do is record a walk-around of the property: This will dramatically increase your interest online because people will have a feeling as if they're already in the house. It will also narrow down the list of people who are actually interested in buying the property because they won't be caught by surprise once they step foot on the property.

Many buyers dislike a home once they're at a showing because they don't know what to expect – they've only seen a few pictures. If a buyer sees a home tour and is still interest, this means they're more likely to purchase the property. Combine aerial videos that your photographer took with their drone and shoot a small 2-3 minute walk around of the property. When you upload the property, list the address and the city/zip code which will gather even more interest by people searching for that location.

Marketing Strategy #5) Create A Dedicated Website

The final step is to make a website for the property. Building a dedicated website might seem like a lot of work, but it's a worthwhile investment compared to simply listing the property on real estate websites. You can use plug-and-play hosting and site builder packages that enable you to create a website on the fly. Your special [yourdomain].com address will certainly be available and a package might cost as little as $10-20 a month. You only have to host a website until the property sells and then you can shut it down.

How to Stage Your Property to Win Over Buyers

Remember when you were a kid and your parents made you clean your room before relatives came over to make a good impression? It's time to put the finishing touches on your property and prepare it for showings – the property has to be in top shape and make buyers feel as if they're already living in it. This is called "staging". The final piece of the puzzle to selling a property is to stage the property for buyers. The realtor will organize "open days" where they pitch the property to multiple people and the interior and exterior have to be in top shape to make an impression. This means no debris from the saw dust your contractor left behind, no yellow patches on the lawn, no unpacked tiles waiting in the bathroom. The property has to be completely furnished, cleaned and ready to show-off. Realtors refer to the whole process as "staging". In many cases you want to stage a property before you start taking pictures and posting it online. Staging is not recommended for all homes: Most low-value flips don't require staging and realtors will skip open days in favor of a quick sale. Staging has to make the home feel as if people will live in it - the key to successful staging is to make it feel like a real home.

Buyers who attend open house days will pay attention to the cleanliness and maintenance level of the property. Two realtors will combine forces and bring over "qualified" buyers who are in the price range of the property, and buyers make impulsive decisions and purchase a property on a whim! This is why making a good first impression is imperative for the sale of the property. Even if you have to pay extra for power-washing and landscaping, it's worth it as it will expedite the sale of the home. The final decision buyers make will always be driven by emotion and if they perceive the house as high-value on arrival, they will be keen to buy it and place higher bids. This helps you because it takes your property off the market, saving you on carrying costs and allowing you to move on to the next property.

How Staging Works: The Basics

Staging works by highlighting the strengths of the house and camouflaging the weaknesses. Appearance is the sole driving factor behind 90% of all purchases in real estate, and the few people who are willing to buy a home that does not visually appeal to them are investors. Although no house is perfect, there are many features you can enhance in a typical house that will showcase the best parts of the house and conceal the worst ones. This usually comes down to smart decisions. **Example**: You have a large window that faces the sunset on the second floor. Don't make the mistake of covering that window and instead showcase it as a highlight. Add or remove furniture that enhances the size of the room.

Staging The Interior

To stage areas of the house such as the kitchen, you can either fully replace the outdated kitchen with a new turnkey kitchen (that can run up to $20,000) or you can simply replace appliances. A much faster way to stage a kitchen is to purchase new stainless steel appliances that will create a clean and crisp appearance for your buyers. The same applies for the living room: If you attach a shiny new plasma screen, this will give the living room an appearance of luxury and modernity.

Staging The Exterior

If the home has a large back yard with its own patio or deck area, don't leave it empty! Purchase a few solid chairs and a table in order to allow buyers to visualize their life and all the memories they could make in that back yard. The buyers have to picture themselves grilling there, playing with their kids and spending time with their family. To make that happen, purchase the furniture you need and facilitate these experiences. If the lawn is in bad shape, hire a landscaper who will spend a few hours fixing the "bald" spots on the grass and consider hiring painters who can paint the yellow grass green.

Staging Tip #1: Furniture Arrangement

Reconsider the furniture placement in the living room and bedrooms - buyers will analyze the space to sense whether they have enough space to comfortably move around the area. Arrangement is key here - make sure the sofas and chairs are placed in a way that enables conversation. If the room feels cluttered, dump the furniture in the trash. Many times you need a minimalistic design with the main sofa, a table and some side chairs. Focus on "conversational" alignment of furniture. Can the living room comfortably fit 5-10 people who are having a conversation? If the answer is no, purchase the furniture or re-arrange it in a way that enables conversation.

Staging Tip #2: Opening Up Space

Many small rooms such as the second room can feel cramped - to create an open feeling, move the furniture right next to the walls. This will open up the empty space and enlarge the space in the room. The opposite applies for large rooms - if there's too much space, pull the furniture towards the middle of the room which will free up space between the furniture and the walls. In both cases re-arranging can open up the space and show people that the rooms have space for movement.

Pro Tip: Furniture should indicate the way traffic in the rooms moves. Focus on creating fluid walking space where the person won't have to think about bouncing over pieces of furniture. Buyers should be able to navigate around large pieces of furniture such as beds and sofas.

Staging Tip #3: Buying Accessories

Invest in accessories such as flowers and books to enhance the sense of comfort in a room. If the rooms feel too "empty" you can purchase flowers and carefully place them on the tables or near the walls where they enhance the homely feeling of the property. Accessories should determine the purpose of a room. **Example**: The exterior should have relaxing rocking chairs where the residents can relax. The living room should have a main table and a place for books. Most accessories are inexpensive and universally-appealing, making the home more desirable for buyers.

Chapter 8 - Staying Smart

House-Flipping Mistakes to Avoid at All Costs

Think your $50,000 renovation budget couldn't flop? Even if you under-spend on your renovations, there are "red-flags" you should avoid before and after the purchase of a property. Details, details, details! When you're buying a house, when you're talking to contractors, buying insurance, sending inspectors and renovating you have to pay attention to the following "red flags" that could signal your property is going to flop in advance. The impact of failure under each one of these could reflect in tens of thousands of dollars lost on your bottom line. The two biggest problems you'll run into are acquisition price and contractor losses, and both will lay on your consciousness. The first problem is related to the purchase price: If you purchase a home for more than your initial budget, you will have less money for renovation which leaves you with little/no profits at the end. If you don't investigate your contractors and they do a sloppy job, you will have trouble selling the property at the end of each renovation.

1) Over/Under Renovating A Property

Example: If a property needs $30,000 in renovations: $10,000 for a bathroom, $10,000 for a kitchen and $10,000 spread over other miscellaneous costs - you shouldn't spend $50,000 (over-spending) or $15,000 (under-spending): You have to invest that exact amount! Focus on the upgrades the home desperately needs. Is the kitchen in good shape but the bathroom is falling apart? Spend 50% of your budget on the bathroom and spend less on the kitchen - it makes no sense to invest equally if one room is in worse shape than another. Things can get expensive fast: Something as simple as smart fridge can end up costing you thousands of dollars. Maybe skip working on the back yard and focus on the interior. Seek out lower cost tiles and floors. Buy cabinetry on sale. Buyers can't tell a difference between a $5/sq ft. floor and $10/sq ft. floor - this could make a huge difference in your bottom line. Keep the renovations "easy" by focusing on the basics i.e. cosmetic repairs. The second you go into structural issues, roofing, foundation work - those are not "easy" fixes and your budget will be overblown fast.

Visit trade shows or "open houses" where you can see new suburban developments: What do they have on the inside? Check out their HVAC system, plumbing, electrical setup, kitchen appliances, etc. If investors are spending millions of dollars on developments they are making those bucks back big-time. This means their houses are trendy and you can copy directly for your property. To "wow" your future customers you should invest in small-time smart appliances such as thermostats, security systems and LED fixtures. This will solidify the value of your smart upgrades.

2) Taking Bigger Projects Than You Can Afford

If this is your first flip, start with small homes and never spend more than $40,000 on a renovation. Your magic number is $40,000 - this is enough to renovate most average homes in the United States. Spread that budget to $15,000 for bathrooms, $15,000 for the kitchen and $10,000 for minor purchases. If you start out with $100,000 renovations you will be overwhelmed by the sheer scope of the work and the management levels you'll have to put in at that level of rehab.

Progressively carry out bigger renovations to make bigger margins once you're fully aware of the risks involved and day-to-day dealings with contractors. Example: A large rehab might require tearing down a wall to open up the kitchen area to the living room. What happens when you tear down the wall? You have to purchase additional reinforcements, you discover molding, some termites can hide below the wall, and now you're paying for 5 other things at once (that you didn't calculate in your initial budget). All these issues can extend the time it takes to renovate and sell. If you focus on renovations under $40,000<, you're putting yourself at minimal risk and you're almost guaranteed to sell.

Cosmetic repairs under $40,000 are "easy" and will familiarize you with repairs on all levels: You'll know how to carry out kitchen, bathroom and flooring repairs. You'll know how to fix the exterior and make the house have curb appeal. You'll know how to install security systems. This is when you'll be ready to move on to bigger upgrades such as changing the foundation, tearing down walls, joining rooms together, adding space/garages, and even adding/removing entire floors.

3) Forgetting To Network

The real-estate business is old-fashioned and people value "connections": You'll need a network of like-minded professionals who can help you flip your properties and act fast. What happens when you run into a sudden problem such as with bathroom tiles and you need a second sub-contractor? You could simply call your real-estate buddy and he will refer you to the adequate sub-contractors because he's ran into a similar problem before. The biggest pitfall before starting is not networking: Spend a month attending networking events and conferences before your first flip. Make friends in the business and visit their construction sites to offer them a hand. Once you have friendships you have people to rely on for advice and connections if you ever run into problems (which you will!).

4) Not Inspecting The House Before Purchase

The appraiser and realtor have to take a detailed look at the existing infrastructure to inform you of every upgrade you have to make - don't purchase a house before a detailed analysis. Many novice flippers are shy or over-confident and they think because a property is cosmetically in good shape that it's not going to require major upgrades. The appraiser has to take a detailed look at the HVAC system, plumbing, electrical, roof/structural shape, fireplace, and more to make sure the infrastructure of the home is on solid shape. Carefully evaluate the upgrades necessary because those will reflect in your renovation budget which has a direct impact on the net profit you're left at the end of each sale.

5) Overpaying For Houses

Let's say a home is worth $80,000 based on the appraisers/realtor's information but the seller asks for $90,000 - you should refuse to pay. Many novice flippers are driven by emotion and think because they ran into a good deal once, that they won't run into a good deal again. You tell yourself "So what, it's only $10,000!" but at the end of the day that money could have went in your pocket if you simply moved on. Remember that the purchase price can have a significant impact in the net profit you take home – the purchase price can affect this as much as the renovation cost. Calculate how much you can spend by estimating the ARV and the 70% rule and don't overbid a single cent. You should actually be down-bidding sellers the same way buyers will try to do once you sell your property. Remember the rule: Pay less, make more.

6) Forgetting To Increase Coverage Insurance

The second you renovate a home, immediately call your insurance provider and ask for additional coverage. Home insurance plans insure a home at 100% of the home value. What happens when you carry out renovations and the home value increases by 30%? You need an additional 30% coverage to cover up that spike. If you fail to increase the insurance and something happens to the home, you will lose significant money. As soon as you make renovations, you must rush to the insurance office to increase coverage on the home based on the new estimated value.

7) Not Screening Contractors

Think checking licenses and bonding is enough? No! You must thoroughly investigate each contractor as if you're stalking them: Call up their previous references, visit current construction sites they're working on, check their portfolio and visit those properties, read reviews on Angie's List and Google them to verify there aren't any horror-stories of investors dealing with those contractors. Once you've checked and verified their reliability, that's when you sign the contract. You can't trust a contractor with tens of thousands of dollars on blind faith. You want to make sure your investment is safe in their hands and the only way to do that is due-diligence research.

8) Hiring Overly Cheap Labor

What if you hire a cheap contractor and you discover badly placed cabinets in the kitchen with cigarette buds left all over the house? What if the contractor delays the work indefinitely but they take your money in advance? There are many things that can go wrong with cheap labor. Always opt for "average" contractors that have good reviews. The best contractors will over-charge you for basic work. The cheapest contractors tend to be unreliable (the work has to be re-done). Average contractors get the job done and they expect regular compensation. There are certain exceptions: If a lawyer is starting out at $20/hour you'll be suspicious because many lawyers charge 10x as much. However, if they want to build up their name they will be willing to work for next to nothing. Take advantage!

The aforementioned factors could affect your bottom-line by tens of thousands of dollars - be cautious! You can overspend at every milestone of the house-flipping business: Make sure each dollar you invest has a multiplying factor (for each dollar you invest you want to get at least two dollars back!).

4 Warning Signs Your House-Flip is Flopping

You're in the middle of a flip – what could go wrong that you can't plan in advance? If the windows won't open, if the door handle is jammed, if the paint-job feels off, there are many things that you will discover "in the moment" that you couldn't pre-meditate and you must fix right then and there. This is what we call "warning signs": Problems that pop-up mid-construction that you must calibrate for in the moment and solve them immediately. In most cases you notice warning signs when it's too late.

Example: A contractor finishes flooring and the floor is uneven. You then have to take out the uneven section or cover it up some way. You must learn from experience by making mistakes and fixing them. Most mistakes will not be your fault but the fault of the contractor. Even though 80% of all renovations go smoothly, the 20% can be a nightmare if you're on a tight budget and have to repeat a major job.

Flipping Houses

Don't blame yourself because even an experienced contractor can mess up once in a while. Be cautious of the following warning signs during your renovation:

Warning Sign #1) Doors/Windows Won't Open

The biggest and most common renovation problem is a lack of careful placement of doors and windows. Many laborers will rush to "get the job done" and misalign the positioning or get the angles wrong. This way, you as the resident can't enjoy a casual walk through your home. **Example**: The handle on the door doesn't latch securely (loose bolts). The door doesn't close smoothly due to a bad angling. The door doesn't clutch property once it's locked but small pressure can open it. The same applies for windows: A small millimeter shift in windows can cause the house to not function as intended, and leak weather such as wind.

Many contractors only replace the door but forget to replace the jamb - this creates serious problems when the two are not aligned properly. To avert that, hire contractors who replace the jamb along with the door. This way everything aligns perfectly once you close the door. If you hire cheap labor you will experience a lot of sloppy work on details like these. The door and door frame have to square up for the job to be considered successful. Double-check to make sure the windows open and close properly. Test all the clutches. Contact the contractor and demand solutions if something goes wrong - you paid them.

Warning Sign #2) Bad Work In The Kitchen

Remember the phrase: "The kitchen is the heart of the home". The kitchen will sell your home and attention to detail in the kitchen is imperative. Your contractor must align the kitchen layout in a functional manner. If you have a bad layout in the kitchen, you can't camouflage that by purchasing shiny steel appliances and new granite countertops. The first thing you'll notice when you enter a badly-renovated kitchen is that the appliances aren't laid out correctly. There will also be gaps between the countertops and new doors that are badly installed on old cabinets. Good contractors will organize the "invisible" side of the kitchen as well. For example, under the kitchen sink you usually have the dishwasher connector, sink drains and garbage disposal at the same time. Make sure they don't interfere with each-others functioning and/or remove certain parts from there appropriately.

Warning Sign #3) The HVAC System Is Dirty

HVAC: Short for "Heating, Ventilating and Air Conditioning" is the temperature-management system of the house. The HVAC system is the key to any comfortable home. However, many times you can't see the debris that piles up in the house system during repairs which lasted for months. If the renovation lasted half a year, you have a lot of garbage to remove and must hire an adequate sanitation crew for the HVAC system. The HVAC is a nest for airborne bacteria and drywall dust. Put your finger on the blower fan blades and notice if they're full of drywall dust. If your finger is covered in the dust, this is a very bad sign. Take a look at the evaporator core of the air conditioner and get a professional crew to clean it at the end of renovation. This is going to be a cheap but significant renovation. Buyers might think the home is in top shape by looking at the cosmetic repairs you've made, but there are underlying repairs that you have to carry out for their own good which are invisible.

Warning Sign #4) The Flooring Is Uneven

There's no bigger warning sign than looking down and seeing uneven patches at the ground level - this is how you know your contractor screwed up! If you want to assess how fast your property will flip, take a look at the state of the flooring. If the flooring is butted up to base molding you must cut out the bottoms and remove the molding on the base. Once that's done, you can lay the flooring again.

In many cases mold will build up fast and you have to re-do the job. The flooring has to look right at the trim edges of the home because this is the first thing buyers will buy once they review the property. If the buyers notice poor flooring, this will be an indicator that the home was redone by clumsy contractors and they will assume the home has more serious problems such as electric work and plumbing that need to be fixed.

4 Exit Strategies to Always Keep in Mind

You put tens of thousands of dollars in a property, the renovations were carried out and it's about to sell. What happens if the house doesn't sell? What are the "last resort" strategies you can implement to prepare for a worst-case scenario? In house flipping, these are called "exit strategies". If a flip goes wrong, if everything falls apart, you must have an "exit strategy" to save your money and get out. Many FSBO listings fail due to a lack of marketing, no connections to realtors, bad renovations or all of the above. Focus on not over-spending money on your renovations for a start. If your renovation budget is $40,000, don't over-spend by a cent. Try to lower your contractor expenses in advance, which ensures that if you do end up with surcharges you will afford it using the leftover cash. If you spend recklessly you will end up going over-budget on your renovation and this might delay your sale as you'll have to sell for higher than you initially calculated to break even. Most house-flips end up profitable and/or the flipper makes their money back in the least.

Pro Tip: Don't panic - You're safe. Once you've purchased a property you have an asset that you can re-sell even without renovating it. You can never fall too low unless you recklessly spend on upgrades that are not necessary.

Exit Strategy #1) Lower The Price

We don't like hearing it - the worst thing a realtor can say to a seller is "lower your price". However, this method is the fastest exit strategy to get out of a bad house flip. If the contractors messed up and you don't have time to re-do the jobs, simply lower the asking price and you'll probably sell the home in the first few weeks. If your property is worth $200,000 and your net profit is $20,000, it might be worth lowering that to $190,000 and only ending up with $10,000 profit rather than waiting for months to sell the property at the $200,000 price tag.

This way you can "get out" of a bad deal and move on to better properties with better contractors. Time is of the essence here, especially on borrowed money. Every day that your house sits on the market increases your cost and you'll be spending thousands in insurance premiums that probably spiked after you renovated the property. Lesser profits are a better option than staying on the market for half a year. Remember that your time is precious and once you get out you can take the lessons you learned from this property and apply them on the next one to make more profits. If you're reading this in advance, be cautious with your ARV estimates and nail your ARV up front to avert drastic exit strategies.

Lowering the price means accepting the loss and proceeding to do better. You will learn a lot by making lesser profits if your renovations failed due to bad contractors and/or side issues that you never expected. Even experienced flippers have issues that come up at the random. Accept the loss and make the next one a win! Remember that timing is important. If you spent only 3 months buying, renovating and selling you would be able to move on a lot faster. You're not emotionally attached to a property that you spent only a few months renovating. You will have at least 3 more tries to get this right in the same year. Whatever failed or went wrong that disallows you to sell the house at full ARV price, don't repeat that mistake again. You'll be smarter this time.

Exit Strategy #2) Offer A Lease

You have a motivated buyer looking to buy at full price - problem is, they can't afford a mortgage yet. The "lesser" is the seller (you) and the "lessee" is the person purchasing a property from you on an extended contract. They will be able to afford a mortgage 6 or 12 months down the line once they get a promotion, gather more money for a down payment, etc. In leasing, the buyer will be able to put down some deposit that you collect at the start of the lease. The deposit then secures their right to buy the property at an agreed date further down the line. This gives you some "get out" cash and security that you've found a buyer. You'll be able to feel some of the profits right away.

Flipping Houses

Leasing implies that you both agree to certain "lease terms" - the buyer will be paying you a monthly leasing fee on top of the rent that will increase your cash flow and give them time to gather money for a full mortgage that will pay off the house and give you back your investment. Leasing is even smarter option than renting because the tenant has much higher interest in the property and agrees to purchase it at a fixed date. Their "investment" in the property means they'll take much better care of the property as they plan to live there forever. The initial down-payment/deposit on a lease should be at least 5 figures: $10,000-50,000 depending on the price of the house. This deposit is non-refundable.

It's legal to collect an "option down payment" which is the advance payment the lessee pays for living in the property. However, if they change their mind about the purchase of that property they will not be entitled to a refund. You will need a real estate attorney that can draft up the contracts that protect you against lessees who change their mind. This is a method employed by people who either expect to make more money in a certain time period that will allow them to buy the house outright, and it's used by people who already have access to capital but their credit rating is bad and they're not eligible for a mortgage. In many cases credit rating can be affected not only by reckless spending but simply a bankruptcy such as a divorce, death and/or health issues. There can be many scenarios why a person's credit was affected but they are still on the market to buy a home - you only have to give them the time to gather the money to fund a full purchase. You can charge them rent fees on top of the advance lease fee. This is the best exit strategy for people who don't want to lower their price on the sale but have time and want to solve the problem on a long-term basis.

Exit Strategy #3) Become A Landlord

The good old land-lord strategy is the go-to for people who don't want to settle for lesser prices and are heavily invested in a project. If your home value is $500,000 you probably don't want to let it go for $450,000 just to make a quick sale. In this event, the rent income you collect can cover your mortgage, utility bills, insurance, taxes and even leave you with some profits at the end to finance further deals. Rental income is serious business and many people specialize in buying cheap properties only to rent them out - not to sell. It's possible to rent the home and list it on the market at the same time, allowing you to collect income while you're trying to cash out on the big sale. If your loan has high interest rates the last thing you want is to default on that loan and get the property taken away from you after you've renovated it!

Pro Tip: It's much easier to rent a house than to sell it. You can find tenants for the house in as little as a week and once you sign a lease for 3 months or 6 months you can still show the property to potential buyers and tell them the move-in date if they're interested in purchasing. If you want to save money, rent out the home immediately and start marketing the home as a "for sale" home online. This way you will have a steady income that covers your carrying costs on top of offers from buyers. There is also a psychological side benefit: If buyers see people are already living in the home, they will associate this with a "finished" home and not something you renovated for a quick profit.

Research the local market. Is this an owner's market or a renter's market? Take a look at each individual house in the neighborhood and consult with the tenants to determine if they own those houses or if they're renting. Many markets are hot rental markets that you can take advantage of because people will always be looking to rent there. **Example**: If a property is located next to a Corporate HQ you will find many local workers who want to be in proximity of their job but don't want to buy a house yet. This opens up your property to a pool of potential renters who will find it easy to make payments and you'll collect rent each month.

This way if you're paying off your mortgage on a hard money loan or a private money loan, you'll be able to pay off the 8% interest rates easily until you sell the property at full price. Renting property is the way you can keep a property on the market without harming your pockets. If the mortgage, insurance and utility bills amount to $500-

Flipping Houses

800 a month and you rent the property for $1500-2000 a month, you'll be left with $1000 in net profits at the end of each month. Unless you're on the clock and your deal was financed by a private lender who expects you to sell the house, banks won't care if you rent the house as long as they get their monthly payment.

Exit Strategy #4) Wholesale To Investors

The reverse of wholesaling a property at the starting point is to wholesale the property at the end point - many investors will be looking for new properties and you can wholesale the property to them to get out immediately. The new investor will pay off your initial investment and renovation value and they'll sell the property themselves. The main reason to wholesale a property instead of lease or rent out is if you're tied between multiple properties and you don't have time to deal with individual buyers/renters who you have to deal with every month. If you're financing 5 properties at the same time and one doesn't seem to go right, the best way to get out of it is to wholesale it to a different investor who is more motivated to take over this property. This way, you get your "get out" paycheck and the new investor gets a new property.

Conclusion – The Takeaways

We promise you this: Every morning you'll wake up excited. Once you've bought your first house and the renovations start, you'll wake up and rush to the construction site trying to get your hands dirty like you're about to move in there! House-flipping is an adrenaline-induced journey where you realize you're on the brink of making a huge profit and you're seeing your investments materialize in front of your own eyes. There are few feelings that can compare to a successful flip, once you've done all the work and put the finishing pieces together - you can do it.

We want to give you encouragement. You're in this for the long haul. If you start today, remember it might take you 3 months until you get to the first stages of flipping. That's the best case scenario. The average flip takes 6 months. Take your time and consider each step of the way carefully - and cross-reference the value points in this book every time once you run into trouble and need help. You'll forget most things we talked about, but as you gain experience you will internalize the lessons and flipping will become second nature.

We presented the nitty-gritty details you need to battle it out in the world of house-flipping. You now know how to pick properties, finance 6-figure deals, carry out renovations start-to-finish and finally market/sell houses to buyers. It's up to you to decide what to make of this information. You may act on this information today or postpone it and act 5 years from now when you're ready. The information will hold true then still - house-flipping has been around for decades and the same principle and methods apply.

In 6 Months You'll Be A Different Person

Take it slow - you're at the baby stages of house-flipping. You have a long way to go until your first "Sold!" sign. If you're nervous, it's normal because your life is about to change. One day you'll be calling realtors or property owners and buying your first home. 6 months from now you'll be shaking the hands of a new buyer who bought your home! You'll experience those initial "awkward" conversations when you try to convince sellers to give you a low price on their property. Maybe you'll dislike the sellers you're calling up or and maybe you won't like the properties once you step foot on them in person. Maybe the sellers will be great and you'll be eager to buy their properties. Congratulations – you've become a property owner!

You'll eventually have the pleasure of dealing with the "finance" people who will finance your whole flip: They'll provide the money for acquisition and bankroll the renovations. It's on you to estimate the repairs, run your calculations, decide the ARV, and spend that money adequately. You'll have to hire contractors and meet them in person: Scary business! You'll then watch people working for you and signing off their checks. Maybe you don't need contractors and want to get your hands dirty yourself? The buyers won't care if you did it yourself or hired a contractor as long as their property is renovated to their taste. Are you an experienced contractor who wants to get his foot in the flipping business? No one will be more competent at this job than you – once you finance the initial deals, you'll know how to manage a team of contractors under your wing.

Don't Waste Time - Start Now!

Even if you're only 12 months away from gathering the finances for your first down payment, time is invaluable. Make the first move and start visiting houses in your area "For Sale" and talking to realtors. Attend networking invents and meet like-minded people. Set the foundation and do the groundwork that would allow you the possibility of flipping houses in the first place. If you have little money to invest, work two jobs and gather the finances you need to put down the first down payment. Discover "deals" in your area and try to get in touch with investors who can finance those deals outright.

Start joining networking events, make connections on LinkedIn where you can communicate with real estate investors, attend construction sites and offer them a help in exchange for knowledge. You'll be surprised at how willing people are to help a young grasshopper. The more time you spend at the construction site, the more you'll be confident when it's your turn to flip. Offer value at each step: Pay people in cash for insider knowledge in your area. Offer free labor to an investor who needs help on his flip. They will share their knowledge with you and repay you once you start flipping and run into trouble.

Invent Your Own Method - Flip Your Own Way!

Finally, take the lessons you learned in this book and apply them your way: Invent your own method! It's important to determine how you like to get things done. Some flippers prefer short 3-month flips and make it their goal to flip a property in under 3 months. Others like to take a year and flip an expensive property for a large paycheck at the end of the year. The same principles apply to large-scale construction: Once you're familiar with house-flipping you can move on to bigger deals such as residential buildings and commercial buildings. Hiring contractors works on the same principle – it's only scaling up.

Maybe you like to furnish your properties with luxurious interiors. Make that your signature style of flipping. Maybe you only replace the basics and save money on every flip. Whichever "style" works for you can be replicated on multiple flips in the same year. Most flippers "go with the flow" and renovate each property on an individual basis. Everything could work in theory - find what works for you in practice. You could take over the whole process and carry out the renovations yourself. You could market the home yourself instead of hiring realtors. You could hire GC's and never actually set foot on the property. You could hire realtors and let them sell for you. All of those lead to the same result – a sold house. You'll be glad once your hand is graced with a 6-figure check and a "Sold!" sign – all that hard work will pay off in the end.

FINANCIAL FREEDOM INVESTING

Latest Reliable & Profitable Income Streams. How to Never Be Broke And Create Passive Incomes: Stocks, Bonds, Day Trading, Dividends, Real Estate and Budgeting

Table of Contents

Introduction **123**

Chapter 1: The Building Blocks of Financial Freedom **127**
- *Important Mindset Shifts to Start Accruing Wealth* *127*
- *Essential Steps for Achieving Financial Freedom* *129*
- *How to Set Your Financial Goals* *132*
- *Setting Your Short-Term and Long-Term Goals* *137*
- *10 Ways to Get Out of Debt ASAP* *138*

Chapter 2: How to Budget the Right Way **143**
- *How to Find a Budget That Works for You* *143*
- *6 Must-Know Budgeting Methods to Never Lose Track of Money Again* *145*
- *Which Budget Is Right for You?* *150*
- *7 Ways to Make Budgeting More Enjoyable* *151*
- *7 Important Steps for Building Good Credit* *156*

Chapter 3: Investing 101 .... **161**
- *Types of Investments to Add to Your Portfolio* *161*
- *Tips on Choosing the Right Stocks for You* *170*
- *What Is an Investment Plan?* *174*
- *The 5 Best Stock Trading Strategies of All Time* *175*
- *8 Worst Investing Mistakes to Avoid* *177*

Chapter 4: Dividend Stocks **180**
- *When a Company Pays Dividends* *180*
- *Different Types of Dividends* *181*
- *Choosing Stocks That Pay High Dividends* *185*
- *How to Find the Best Dividend Stocks for Your Portfolio* *187*

Do Not Make These 10 Dividend Investing Mistakes............................ 188

What You Need to Know About Dividend Tax Rates............................ 192

Ordinary vs. Qualified Dividends.. 192

Chapter 5: Day Trading.. 195

What Is Day Trading? 195

How to Start Day Trading 197

Day Trading Strategies 201

Chapter 6: Real Estate Investing 207

Increasing Your Property Value.. 207

Making Money From Rental Property 208

How to Select a Target Market... 216

10 Important Features of Profitable Real Estate 222

Top 15 Real Estate Investing Strategies....................................... 225

Chapter 7: Other Ways to Grow Wealth 228

How to Start Investing in Exchange-Traded Funds (ETFs)................ 228

Start Making Money Now with Peer-to-Peer Lending 231

The 10 Best Strategies for Trading Cryptocurrencies...................... 233

7 Must-Have Apps for Modern-Day Investors 237

Conclusion.. 241

Financial Freedom Investing

Introduction

All of us seek financial freedom for different reasons. It could be that you want this freedom so that you can secure enough money to live comfortably in your retirement years. Others may be looking to purchase a new home, and still others may be planning a nest egg for their later years.

Planning how you will support yourself in your retirement can be stressful, and most people have money concerns looming over their heads. How many times have you turned on the news only to hear that some wealthy individual has just filed for bankruptcy? You might be wondering, *If he can't manage it with all his money, then what chance do I have?*

It is a legitimate concern. A look back through our recent history tells us that times have changed. We can no longer rely on job security to carry us through our lives. Jobs that you could stay on for 30 years or more and retire on a handsome pension plan are now few and far between. If we want financial freedom in this modern world, we need to learn how to think differently.

The challenge that we all face is how to get that financial security without relying on the traditional methods past generations took for granted. Those days are over, and we all need to plan our financial future more creatively.

Financial Freedom Investing

In such situations, it can be difficult to know where to start. Maybe you're thinking about investing, but you don't know enough about it to make wise decisions. You're afraid of losing your hard-earned money on a high-risk gamble. Or maybe you're just tired of living paycheck to paycheck and you see that you need to think differently.

Or you're getting older and your body doesn't want to work as hard as it has before. Whether you're getting up in years and planning for retirement or you're just starting out and you're saving for a big purchase or investment, it makes sense that you start here with us.

There are many ways that we can meet this challenge. We have all learned how difficult it is to just put your money in a savings account and wait for it to grow. The interest rates they offer is such a pittance that you probably feel like you're actually paying the bank to hold your money rather than making anything off of it.

If you've thought about any of these things before, then you've come to the right place. You will be joining many others of like minds who have the same questions. In the following pages, we will show you how you can achieve a level of financial wealth that will put you on a sure footing, where you won't have to worry about your finances. Here, you will find:

- A beginner-friendly guide to investing and various investment options
- Ideas for how to make more money without much extra work needed
- Tips on making both short- and long-term goals and why they are important
- Essential information that can apply to a wide variety of financial needs.

Financial Freedom Investing

There are plenty of alternatives to growing your cash and setting up a secure future for yourself. The answers are out there for anyone who has the wherewithal to look. They are not new, magical, or even mystical. This book is designed specifically to teach you some of those alternatives and how utilizing them can make a huge difference in helping you to achieve your financial freedom.

We've been taught that the fastest way to any destination is in a straight line. Unlike savings, however, this is not always the case. Investing requires that you take a few turns here or there and you may very well hit a few bumps in the road along the way. But, if you stay the course, your investment decisions could easily help you achieve financial freedom much sooner than you might think.

Once you apply the principles in this book, the rewards for your hard work will definitely be worth it. You will have:

- Freedom from money worries
- Freedom from debt
- Freedom to do what you want
- Freedom from painful anxiety
- A better relationship with money
- Freedom to live a life based on your values
- More confidence in your ability to manage money
- Less stress, which means better health
- Freedom to grow wealthy on your own terms

If you're ready to change your life for the better — to stop merely existing in this world rather than truly living — then it is time for you to take the next step. The sooner you start, the sooner you will see yourself journeying that road to financial freedom. It is my responsibility to guide you step by step to that dream lifestyle you want.

Financial Freedom Investing

So, if you're ready to change your life, and move onto something that's even better, then it's time to download this book today. It's totally up to you to take back control of your life and actually win the rat race for a change. So, what are you waiting for? Now is the time to change your life for the better by letting us help you to gain financial freedom.

Financial Freedom Investing

Chapter 1: The Building Blocks of Financial Freedom

Most goals should have a specific end date, but things aren't so simple when it comes to money. For one thing, your ultimate goal of financial freedom needs to be broken down into a lot of smaller goals. Not only that, you will have to live life in a very specific way in order to maintain those circumstances after you have acquired it.

Overwhelmed? Don't be, as it all starts simply by having a specific mindset.

Important Mindset Shifts to Start Accruing Wealth

There is nothing unique about finances. While it may be elusive to some people, it is really just a matter of mastering the fundamentals. Whether you're Jeff Bezos or you're the cleaning lady, the rules of the game are exactly the same: mastering the fundamentals and consistently applying them.

This is not just about saving up for a new car or for a fabulous vacation one day. Yes, savings is very important in the grand scheme of things, but saving just for the sake of saving is not always your best option. Your first goal is to make the most of your money, not just for today or the next few years, but for the remainder of your life. This requires a huge shift in perspective. You're in it for the long haul and that means that what you need for today may not be what is needed in 10 years or 20 or 50.

Financial Freedom Investing

Have you ever heard of people who seem to have struck it rich overnight? Chances are you have. You might even have personally known a few of them. Some of them may have been positioned in high paying jobs where they could sock away a lot of cash whenever they wanted, but others may have started with little or nothing. They may have been the local garbage collector, the housekeeper, or a waitress at a nearby diner.

Aside from those who have acquired their wealth by winning the lottery, others have managed to achieve their money seemingly without effort. However, if you look closely, their imagined overnight success came after years of careful planning. There is nothing more important to your success than changing your mental mindset. You will have to switch from the common ideas that are the norm in today's society to something that will guarantee that you get improved results.

Essential Steps for Achieving Financial Freedom

1. **Make a detailed plan**

   One of the first steps you must do is to create a plan. Your success should not be something you get by accident or by surprise. Each step of your path should be made and achieved by design. Rather than allowing things to just happen, start thinking about everything you do and any possible consequences that can occur.

   Imagine designing your dream home. You've probably thought about it for years. You know every detail, down to the shape and design of each knob and fixture. If it's truly your dream house, you've already thought about what it will take to repair it when things go wrong, what colors to paint it and how often. You know which rooms to give your kids and every feature you'll have in your kitchen.

   You have to take the same extra care when planning for your financial future. You're not thinking just for today but are planning for the future. How many years will it take for you to reach your goal and the kind of effort you will need to maintain it? With a detailed plan, you'll know what to do today, tomorrow, next month, next year, and each year after that. You'll keep doing this until you reach a point where your money will start to work for you.

2. **Get out of the paycheck-to-paycheck mindset**

   We've been programmed from childhood to think in terms of survival. Perhaps it's human nature, but many of us who are struggling to survive tend to focus on the negatives. Even though events may not have automatically come to mind, it's easy to fall into the sky is falling approach to everything. The problem with this line of thinking is that it limits us. When you are concerned, your mind focuses on holding onto every penny you have, investment opportunities can easily pass you by because you're only thinking in the moment.

Wealthy people do not think this way. Because they have a plan, their minds are focused on the next step, which will automatically lead them to prosperity. Their minds are free to explore other possibilities, and they see opportunities all around them. They examine each one and process every aspect of it until they reach a breakthrough where they can see how to use it to grow what they have rather than holding onto everything they have earned.

3. **Don't always play it safe**

In line with the survival line of thinking is the need to seek security. Yes, money can bring you a level of security. You know that if you have enough money, you have a roof over your head, food in your stomach and clothes on your back. However, if your mind never looks beyond your safety net, you may miss many profitable opportunities. No one ever achieved financial independence while sitting on the fence. Playing it safe cuts you off from many avenues you can take to wealth.

This doesn't mean that you should throw caution to the wind. You still need to think things through and analyze every opportunity to make sure that it's a risk that will pay off in the end. Being a risk-taker doesn't mean being foolhardy. It means that you're going to have to step out on faith and believe in your decisions even when you don't know the outcome.

Courage has been defined as the willingness to take action when you cannot control the outcome. Take the time to read a few background stories of successful people that you admire, and you'll find the same pattern. They recognized an opportunity and took action, often before anyone else saw the potential. By the time others joined in, they were already well on their way to amassing great wealth.

4. Stop thinking about spending and start thinking about saving

This is a mindset that's quite ingrained. If your parents taught you well, then chances are you didn't spend every penny of your allowance when you were a kid. You might have had to save up for that new bike or computer game. Sadly, many young people grow up spending every last penny they have for the things they want. In most cases, the things they want don't last for very long. So, when those things are gone, so is their money.

The average American household spends 110% of their income. When they overspend, they usually find themselves deep in debt with credit cards and loans from friends and family members. If you have a spendthrift attitude, your attempts to acquire wealth will inevitably dig a hole for yourself that will be almost impossible to get out of.

There have been numerous studies that show that you need to save between 20–30% of your income to reach the point where your money will actually work for you. Taking 20% of your income and setting it aside and then living off the rest is not that hard. Once you make this adjustment, you're not likely to even notice the difference.

5. **Stop hoping and start doing**

   Hope is a powerful motivator, but there will always comes a time when you need to take action. You need to stop thinking about what you want to do and become proactive. Even the smallest step in the right direction can be rewarding.

   Most people do not realize that they are paralyzed by hope. They spend their time talking and sharing their ideas, but they rarely get beyond that point. Rather than spending your energy sharing your plans with others, start gathering what you need to execute your plan.

Just like everything else in life, nothing we say or do happens without it first being a thought. If you've developed bad financial habits in the past, they were started with your thinking. So, in order to gain financial freedom, it is necessary for you to change the way you think about money. By changing your thoughts, you can accomplish great things in an amazingly short amount of time. You'll start off slowly at first, but gradually your plans will pick up momentum and as the time passes you see small successes along your path, you'll start to feel more confident and you'll see your freedom just beyond that light at the end of the tunnel.

How to Set Your Financial Goals

Financial Freedom Investing

Most people do not fully understand money or how it works. They think that having cash on hand is security and cannot grasp how saving it may not be the best choice for them. Anything you do to increase your financial security has to have a goal. If you are saving money, you need to have a goal for that. Money is not the end-all of anything you do. It is the means to an end. If money is never used for any purpose, you end up either wasting it on frivolous things or hoarding it. In the end, you may leave this earth and all your money behind for someone else to use.

Take a long hard look at your goals and try to determine where your money should be going. Actually, sitting down and putting pen to paper can be a little scary, but it brings you face to face with your financial realities.

When you're laying out what you plan to do with your money and setting your goals, it can be kind of cathartic. But before you do anything, make sure your boots are firmly planted on the ground. Without clearly defined goals, you may end up jumping ship and splurging the first chance you get. It could be very easy to end up watching that wealth as it slips away, buried under a mountain of debt. So, when setting your goals, start with a realistic but flexible plan. What you might want today may not be what you want later in life, make sure you have some wiggle room to work with.

- **Determine how much money you have to start with.** It doesn't matter if your goals are short or long-term, you need to know your starting point. Be realistic about how much you have to work with. If you don't, it is quite likely you'll work your way to the bottom of your wallet before you reach your final destination. Remember, your goal is to stop living from paycheck to paycheck, so you don't want to start blind.

Take some time to sit down and get a realistic look at your current financial situation. Your starting point should consist of 1) how much money you have on hand and in your bank accounts, IRAs, or investments; include physical assets that you may have already paid off. 2) List all of the debts you still have outstanding. Consider credit card balances, mortgages, student loans, child support or any other financial obligations that you have to meet.

Take the total amount you owe and deduct it from your total assets to get your net worth. This is your starting point. Don't worry if this number is in the negative, the goal of reading this book is to change that.

- **Create a budget.** Now that you know what you're worth financially, you have a starting point and you can figure out a budget. Your budget will be a detailed outline of all the expenses that you have and how much you will pay towards them every month.

- **Make sure you cover everything.** That includes that $10.00/month video streaming service that you take for granted. In addition to obvious expenses, include utilities, insurance policies, food, gas, and entertainment. Don't leave anything out. If you're not sure of what to include on the list, go back over the last few months of receipts and take a look. This list will be the foundation of your budget.

Take a look at your starting figure. If you don't like it, then go back through your list to see if you can cut some of those expenses. What can you eliminate? Cable? Streaming? Subscription accounts? You might even be able to forego eating out and opt to do more cooking at home.

This doesn't mean that you have to give up on your good times, you just have to be willing to sacrifice a little to get better returns. Once you've decided what you can do without, you'll see that final number getting larger. You now have a budget!

Now that you know how much you have to work with, you can start setting realistic goals.

- **Set practical goals.** Financial goals are not the same for everyone, so no one can tell you what to shoot for. However, there are some practical goals you might want to consider. You can always add to them later if you want. The most common goals you'll find people set are:

    o Establishing an emergency fund
    o Getting out of debt
    o Planning for retirement
    o Buying a home or a car
    o Taking a dream vacation

You can choose for yourself which ones should be addressed first, but as long as the first three are addressed you should be able to find the security you're looking for. Follow these basic suggestions to help you get started.

Goal 1: Establishing an emergency fund. If you've done your budget well, you'll at least have a few dollars to dedicate to an emergency fund. In the beginning, it may not be much. Maybe

$5 or $10 each paycheck. However, if you are consistent, you'll be amazed at just how much you can accumulate with a steady deposit of a few bucks into your account.

You decide just how much money you want to have in your emergency fund. No one can tell you how much you need, but a general guideline is three to six months' worth of living expenses should be set aside. If you have good job security that may be enough, but if you're on a precarious footing with your job, then you might decide on a little more.

Goal 2: Pay Down Your Debt. It is easy to get bogged down in bills every month and it can be very discouraging to watch your account bleed out every payday. Some people see money as electricity, and they are merely the wire it passes through. It goes out as fast, if not faster, than its coming in.

The best way to solve this problem is to take aim on those bills and pay them off. Being-debt free may feel like an impossible task, but if you're willing to make a few sacrifices in the beginning, even a few extra dollars added to each payment will start to see that balance slowly begin to. Just make sure that you don't spend any of your emergency fund money in the interim.

Goal 3: Planning for retirement. You want to think about your future, even if you're a long way from its reality. If you haven't thought much about this yet, then you're not alone. If you love your job and can't imagine life without it, then maybe you can get by, but by and large, the majority of people want to see a day when they do not have to get up and trudge to work all day. They want to spend their later years doing the things they love and making the most out of their lives.

The sooner you start this plan, the easier it will be to get to that final day at work when you can claim your life back. It doesn't matter how old you are, it's never too early to start planning for retirement. If you have a job that offers a nice 401(k) plan all the better. However, even if they don't, you can still set aside money for those later years on your own. Your future self will thank you profusely for it.

Setting Your Short-Term and Long-Term Goals

Now for the fun part. Once you've got the adult things out of the way, it's time to think about supporting the kid in you. This is where you decide how you will use that accumulated wealth to enhance your quality of life. Think about the kinds of things that will give you enjoyment and satisfaction in life.

It doesn't matter what your goals are, it's time to start making a list to help you to categorize them in order of importance. Start by making a list of all the things you want to do, then separate them into different categories:

1. **Short-term**: goals that can be filled within just a few years. Vacations, buying a car, or taking a gourmet cooking class.

2. **Long-term**: goals that may take you 10 years or more to achieve. Buying a house or developing rental property.

By detailing your heart's desire on paper, you put them front and center in your life. Make sure when you write down your goals that you also set an estimated timeline for achieving it. The timeline is what will motivate you to move forward, do the necessary research and take the steps to achieve it without procrastinating.

10 Ways to Get Out of Debt ASAP

The fun part of budgeting and financial planning is in your dreams. But if you're serious about obtaining financial freedom you need to get out of debt first. This can be difficult when you consider that most people today are in debt to the tune of nearly $25,000. That's a lot of bills to pay.

Because people tend to spend more than they earn, the accumulated debt in most cases is the result of credit use to make up the difference. If you want to find the wealth you're looking for, you can no longer hide behind your credit to get the things you need. All it takes is one disaster or unfortunate event and you'll be well on your way to bankruptcy.

1. **Don't just pay the minimum payment.** Take a look at the interest rate on your credit card statement. In most cases, it is 15% or higher. At that rate, if you pay only the minimum payment amount each month, it could take you years to pay it off. This is one of the main reasons why people are unable to see their way clear of credit card bills, but interest rates can be the bane of your existence in other loans too. Think about all the interest you're paying for your student loans, personal loans, or other forms of debt.

Financial Freedom Investing

- o The best way to pay these bills down faster is to pay more than the minimum payment. You'll not only cut down on the interest you pay, but the additional money you add will help to reduce the principal amount owed speeding up the payment process.

- o Before you completely pay off your debt, check to make sure that your creditor is not going to charge you any prepayment penalties for paying it off early.

2. **Use the snowball method**. If you can find a way to pay more than the minimum monthly payment, you can use the snowball method to pay off your debts. This will not only get the bills paid, but it will boost your sense of accomplishment along the way.

    - o List all of your debts from the smallest to the largest. Use all your excess funds to pay off the smallest debt first and make minimum monthly payments on all the other ones. Once the smallest bill is paid off, then take that extra cash and pay it towards the next smallest bill on the list until that one is paid in full.

    - o In essence, you are snowballing all of your extra money and pushing towards the total amount you owe until you reach a point when you can say you are debt-free.

3. **Get an extra job**. If you can see your way clear to pick up a few extra dollars with an additional job you can actually put a lot more cash in your pocket to pay off those extra bills. It doesn't have to be a regular job where you have to punch a

clock every day. Nearly everyone has some specialized skill or talent that they can tap into. Picking up a few weekend jobs a month or freelance assignments can go far in putting extra cash in your pocket.

4. **Downsize your life**. If you're really determined, you can cut your expenses down to the absolute minimum, until all your bills are paid in full. This means you will eliminate all extra spending and just use enough money to get by. If this thought is making your heart race too fast, relax a little. This type of budget is not meant to be a lifetime decision but will only be exercised until you become debt-free.

5. **Have a garage/yard sale**. Everyone has a lot of stuff they no longer have any use for. Take some time and go through your garage, closets, basements, and attics to see what you've got stashed away. You know the saying, "one man's trash is another man's treasure." If you find things in your home that you no longer use and have no realistic expectations of using them in the future, you should have no problem coming up with things to sell.

    a. If you don't have time to set up a yard sale, consider taking your things to a consignment shop or sell them online on sites like eBay, Facebook, or Craigslist.

6. **Negotiate a lower interest rate.** If you're struggling with excessively high interest rates, it may be possible to negotiate for a lower rate. Many people do not think to make such a request, but many credit companies are happy to oblige, especially if you have a good relationship with them.

7. **Transfer your balance.** If you have one credit card with an extremely high bill and you're paying high interest rates on top of that, you may be able to transfer the remaining balance to another card with a lower interest rate. There are even some cards that offer a 0% interest rate for the first 18 months. With that kind of kick, you'll have a lot of extra cash to throw at those bills.

8. **Use unexpected money to pay down debt.** Throughout the year, you may receive additional unexpected income. For example, you might receive an end-of-the-year bonus from your employer, or you may get a nice fat tax refund check. Perhaps a rich uncle has left you a tidy little sum or you get a raise. Whatever the case, it is not money that you have dedicated to your budgetary expenses. Use that money to pay down your debt and you'll be well ahead of the game.

9. **Stop unnecessary spending.** More often than not, the credit card balance doesn't go down because you keep adding to it. Taking the time to examine how you use your credit card can give you a good picture of your spending habits. By looking back over your past expenditures, you can decide for yourself if the debt was really worth it. Maybe you could have settled for a regular cup of coffee rather than a mocha Frappuccino. Brown bagging it to work can keep you from going out to eat saving you tons of money. By eliminating expensive habits, you can cut your overall expenses down to something that is much more manageable.

10. **Avoid temptation.** We all have things that are hard to resist. Still, you can almost guarantee that with all the marketing and advertising going on around you every day, the carrot that society is dangling in front of your eyes every day will tempt

you. When you're trying to pay down debt, it is best to try to avoid those temptations wherever you go. If you're drawn into your favorite restaurant on your way home from work every day, try taking a different route. If you see the same tempting commercial on when you watch TV, consider changing the channel or at least getting up and walking out of the room during commercial breaks.

The bottom line is *you have a choice*. You can continue to take the easy road and just stick your head in the sand, pretending you do not see your financial situation, or you can face your debt issues head on. Whether you choose to do it now or are faced to deal with it later, you're going to have to pay your bills. It's better to do it on your own terms.

The main thing to remember is that there is a way out, but don't expect a miracle. With your plans to achieve financial freedom, it's going to take a little hustle on your part, but if you do, you'll be richly rewarded for all your hard work in the end.

Chapter 2: How to Budget the Right Way

Building good credit is essential to your financial future. While it is possible to live in this world without credit, it is not easy. But, getting out of debt and reestablishing your credit is not easy either. It takes careful planning and becoming fully aware off every dollar you spend. The only way to get out of the quagmire is by careful budgeting, but even that can get a little confusing. There are so many different plans for budgeting that it can be overwhelming to know what to do.

The problem is that creating a budget is not as cut and dry as you might believe. Just like not all credit habits are the same, not all approaches to correcting your financial situation will be suitable for you. Yes, the ultimate goal remains consistent: you want to pay down debt, build up a little nest egg, or work towards a major purchase. But reality dictates that there are many roads you can take to get there.

How to Find a Budget That Works for You

Before you can decide on the method that you will apply to your finances, think about the factors that are currently affecting your life. Clearly, a single person living alone will not have as much to worry about as one who has a family to support. You also have to dedicate time to creating a budget and consider the resources you have at your disposal. Below are several budgeting methods you can consider. Read them through and see which one rings true for you. This will help you to determine where you lie on the spectrum so you can plan an effective approach to budgeting going forward.

When you know your starting point, deciding the route to take is much easier. You know what you have to work with and where you want to end up. All that's left is to draw a line on your road map.

1. **Know your values.** Your values consist of what matters to you, the things in your life that you feel you can't live without. Obviously, food, clothing, and shelter would be on the top of this list. Values may differ from person to person. The point is that understanding your values will help you to prioritize what's most important in your budget.

2. **Set your goals.** Your values will give you clear directions on what you should be striving for. Think about what you want your money to do for you in the future, but don't just write down one single long-term goal. Break it up into workable steps. What would you like to accomplish in the next month, three months, six months, a year, three years, five years, 10 years?

3. **Know your income.** How much money do you bring home each pay period – after taxes? This will be the money you will use to determine your spending allowance. You only want to include money that you receive on a regular basis and that you KNOW is coming.

4. **Know your expenses.** Look over your credit card statements, bank records, and store receipts. You can divide your expenses into two categories – fixed and flexible expenses. Fixed expenses would be your rent or mortgage, car payment, credit card bills, and student loans.

Flexible expenses are a little harder to figure out. These include things like food, clothing, entertainment, etc. The cost varies from one month to the next. You may have to calculate the total amount over several months and then come up with a reasonable average.

Don't forget about additional expenses that are easily forgotten. These are those costs that you do not pay with regularity; taxes, insurance, subscriptions, etc.

Now, you have all the tools you need to create a workable budget that will help you to meet your needs.

Now comes the part when you have to decide what method will work best for you.

6 Must-Know Budgeting Methods to Never Lose Track of Money Again

As long as the fundamentals of budgeting are covered — tracking expenses, managing income — you have a little leeway in choosing the budgeting method that works for you. If one of them looks like a good fit, then go for it. There's no harm in switching to another one if you find it doesn't quite meet your needs.

Financial Freedom Investing

1. The Line-Item Budget

The line-item budget is designed for those who have problems with major spending issues. People who use it are those that seriously need to get out of debt and have no problem with putting all of their expenses into workable categories.

This system requires you to categorize your expenses. You can create as many categories as you need to: household expenses, credit card debt, transportation costs, food, clothing, utilities, grooming, you get the idea. Under each category, list all of the expenses you have to pay.

Create three columns, estimated spending, actual spending, and whatever is left over. When you compare each of these columns, you will be able to measure your progress after each pay period.

Next to each item, assign a dollar amount to be paid monthly. As you make each payment, make a note of it and deduct the amount from the total due. It might be helpful to create an additional bill for incidentals, that way, nothing is left out.

This budgeting method is perfect for the person that has the time and the resources to figure out a lot of details and the dedication to do the extra work that is involved.

2. The 50/30/20 Budget

The 50/30/20 budget has guidelines that aren't as meticulous. However, with the 50/30/20 budget, you dedicate 50% of your income to necessary expenses, 30% to things you want, and 20% to savings.

This method is ideal for those who are not comfortable with a strict budget or they don't have a lot of time to dedicate to doing a line-item budget. Still, it is flexible enough that you know exactly how much you can put away and how much you have to spend on your daily needs. The model should be flexible enough to fit in with your lifestyle.

3. Pay Yourself First

The pay yourself first model takes money from your income and put it into a savings account before you pay for anything else. Even though you pay yourself first, you will still need to know just how much money you need to meet your expenses so that you have enough to cover them.

This method works well for those who find themselves at the end of the month wondering where all of their money has gone. At the same time, it doesn't require you to stick to a strict dollar accounting.

It also works well with those who have an inconsistent monthly income. First, take the average of the last six months of income, then total all of your expenses for the same period, and then subtract the expenses from the income. The remainder is what you can dedicate to your savings.

4. The Envelope System

There is another system that works with a little tighter pull on the purse strings. It works well for those who need a little more discipline to get the job done. The envelope system helps you to cut back on spending too much on non-essentials without having to keep track of every penny you spend. It is a basic cash-based approach to budgeting.

Determine a spending limit for each expense. For example, you could create individual budgets for groceries, clothing, and entertainment. At the start of each month, divide all of your money into these smaller budget categories and place it into labeled envelopes. Anytime you need to purchase something from one of those categories, you pay for it out of that envelope. When the envelope is empty, you have exhausted your budget and there is no more money to make any more purchases until the next payday.

This method works well for those who struggle to control their spending habits or are relying too heavily on credit or debit cards to pay for things. They don't realize how much they are spending until all of their money is gone.

5. Zero-Sum Budget

Then there is the zero-based budget, which is particularly good for anyone who has a tendency to overspend without realizing it. With this plan, you will know exactly how every dollar you spend is being used. In other words, every dollar must have an intended purpose before it leaves your hands, you must account for every penny in order for it to work well.

The system works exactly the way it sounds. On the last day of the month, your budget should always equal zero. So, if at the end of the month, you have money left over, you must stop and find a home for that money.

It works for those people who usually have a little extra cash at the end of the month. Without giving the money a job to do, the tendency to use it for unnecessary things can be a problem. It forces you to stop and think practically about how best to use your funds so that they push you closer to your goals.

6. The No-Budget Budget

This method requires you to be aware of your spending habits. Rather than worrying about how much is being spent in each of your categories, you spend based on your values and what's most important to you.

It works well for those who may already be pretty frugal and somewhat disciplined about the money they spend.

Start by creating an outline for everything that you feel comfortable spending your money on. Anything that is not in line with what you feel is important or essential should not make it on this list.

For example, you might be someone who prefers traveling and taking a vacation once or twice a year. Any extra money you have after your needs are met can be dedicated to travel.

Some people may prefer to dedicate their money to their pets, others may want to invest in the stock market, while others may be thinking about becoming an entrepreneur. Your discretionary money can pretty much be dedicated to anything that you think is important and can enhance your life.

Which Budget Is Right for You?

As you can see, there are several different ways to budget for your future. While the end-goal is the same with all of them, only one will fit with your lifestyle and your way of managing money.

To decide which system will work best for you, there are a few things you need to keep in mind.

- How much time do you have to monitor your budget? Some methods are relatively easy and do not require a lot of detailed record-keeping. But others may require elaborate record-keeping with numerous Excel spreadsheets and constantly tracking every penny you spend. If you don't have a lot of time to dedicate to such extensive record-keeping, you might want to start working a budget that has a little more give and take.

- You should also think about how often you should monitor your budget. Those who are pretty confident that their budget is on the right track might review their results on a monthly basis, while others may choose to view it once or twice a year. If you're still trying to get the balance just right, you might be more inclined to review it on a weekly basis or even after every purchase.

At the very least, having a budget allows you to approach life with confidence. You know that you have a plan and a direction you want to go in. Every time you pay a bill, you get a sense of pride that you are one step closer to your goals, and that is worth money in the bank.

7 Ways to Make Budgeting More Enjoyable

There are many benefits to learning how to budget properly, but many of us are gun shy from those arduous days from our middle and high school classrooms. However, with just a few little tips, those boring math classes can be brought to life and you can find out just how much fun you can have crunching those numbers.

1. **Take Advantage of Modern Tech**

If you really aren't good at numbers, take advantage of modern tech. There are plenty of excellent applications that can help you to get your budgeting done with minimal effort. Each one has its own set of features that can be applied to your situation. After a careful search and analysis of the available options, it is possible to find one that will fit your needs.

2. Know Your Goals

The work becomes a lot more interesting when you know why you're doing it. When you start by establishing some clear-cut goals, even if they are small ones, it gives meaning to what you want to do. If you set both long and short-term goals, you'll have certain milestones to achieve and once you've mastered a few of them, you'll find yourself motivated to push forward.

Start by setting up a few easy ones that you know you can achieve, and then watch the magic as it happens. There is nothing more motivating and encouraging than success. The larger goals can be broken up into small steps. Each milestone you pass will help you to see that you are making progress even if the end is months or years away.

3. Give Yourself Rewards

The main reason we do anything is for the rewards. We go to work for the reward of the paycheck, we study hard in school for the reward of a good grade, we do our best in competition for the reward of the prize, and we struggle through relationships for the reward of a happy family life. It just stands to reason that you will work harder when there is something rewarding at the end of the fight.

There are all types of rewards you might give yourself, just make sure that your reward is in line with your goals. You could treat yourself to a night on the town after a completing a full month of budgeting, set aside a little money for a vacation or a weekend getaway, or reward yourself with a new outfit or a pair of shoes.

The main point is that you acknowledge what you have accomplished and be happy about it. Perfection is a good goal to reach, but if it is offered at the expense of your mental and emotional stability, you may reach your goal but there won't be much satisfaction in it.

4. **It's Not Just About You**

Even if you have small children, letting everyone in the family be a part of the solution takes a lot of the burden off of you and can make it much more rewarding. Some people turn budgeting into a game by allowing the children to compete by seeing who can either make the most money on odd jobs or who can save the most.

Just as rewards will work well for you, they'll do wonders to motivate the youngest ones in the family: a trip to the local candy store, something from the ice-cream truck, or a day at the park (that's free!). Remember, a reward for your kids is also a reward for you. It'll be easier to achieve your goals and it will be a major boost to your children's self-esteem. They'll learn good money managing habits and they'll feel like part of the solution rather than the problem.

5. Become More Self-Sufficient

Saving money is not just about shifting dollars from one place to another. While you can save that way, it is a lot more fun to learn creative ways to acquire the things you need without shelling out a lot of cash. There is nothing more rewarding than heading out to your backyard to pick your vegetables for dinner than finding them at your local supermarket.

And the best part of it is that everyone in the family can take part. Your children will learn a valuable and precious skill that will last them a lifetime, and you'll save money at the same time. Once they taste the difference in the foods you grow, they may not want to eat store-bought food ever again.

There are a lot of things you can do to save money. In addition to growing your own food, you can create your own cleaning supplies, learn to sew your own clothes, or even make your own hair products. In fact, if you do well, you may be able to parlay some of that into a side business that will help you to keep you on budget too. What can be better than that?

6. Think Differently About Money

Learn to think of money in a different way. Chances are, you've seen money as a source of stress and anxiety for a while now. The need for money has caused many to fall so far into debt, it's no wonder so many people see it in a negative light.

Now, as you begin to see your money working for you rather than against you, it is possible to view it as a means to an end. As you learn how to prioritize your spending and you see its effects as you pass one milestone after another, you'll see money more as a tool you can utilize to your advantage.

7. **Plan for Early Retirement**

The sooner you start planning for retirement, the sooner you'll be able to see money as a way to make it happen. Think about all the things you can have if you are able to retire early. The time you can spend with your family, the vacations you'll enjoy, the time you'll have to do the things you love, and the stress-free life you will lead.

While budgeting may be a necessity, it doesn't have to be painful or stressful. By coming up with creative ways to make it more interesting, you can ensure your success. Creative budgeting can be a great way to motivate your whole family, friends, and neighbors to help you to achieve your goals without losing your heart in the process.

7 Important Steps for Building Good Credit

Bad credit can be the bane of anyone's existence. It can prevent you from renting a decent place to live, stop you from purchasing a home, cut off your means of education, and it might even be the reason you couldn't get a good job. If you have bad credit, then you already know what this feels like.

It can be very exciting to get that first credit card. Every purchase you make, every late payment, starts to develop into a picture that becomes very hard to erase. Being able to use credit responsibly is one sure way of securing your financial future.

Sadly though, this lesson comes a little too late for most people, and they end up having to rebuild their credit and recover from some painful decisions they have made in the past.

The good news though, is that no matter how bad your credit is today, there are ways to rebuild it and restore your good name. It may take time, but by applying some very basic principles you can establish a good credit history, one that you can be proud of.

Whether you're trying to restore your credit or you're just starting out, keep these little tips in mind to protect your image and make sure that your credit doesn't suffer from bad decisions in the future.

Financial Freedom Investing

1. **Never Borrow More Than You Can Afford**

You received your credit because you were viewed as creditworthy, so don't start off using it with bad spending habits. Make sure that when you use your card you only use it for things you can afford. It can be difficult to resist the temptation to buy things on credit that you can already buy without it, but it is a powerful signal to future creditors that you are being responsible. You'll be glad you were frugal when you can later get those big-ticket items you couldn't get before.

This is also true when it comes to taking out loans. Only borrow what you know for a fact you can pay back within a reasonable amount of time. Take a little time to look over your budget so that you know exactly what you can afford to pay on a monthly basis. If the loan payment amount exceeds that number, don't be afraid to walk away.

2. **Don't Use All of Your Credit**

Just because a creditor gives you a maximum limit, it does not give you carte blanche to use it all. When you max out your credit cards, creditors view it as irresponsible, especially if you're not in the habit of paying off your bill in full every month. Lenders notice that borrowers who max out their credit are usually the same ones that have difficulty paying off their balance. Try to keep your balance at around 40% of your credit limit to maintain a good credit score.

3. Don't Get a Lot of Credit Cards

Opening up too much new credit too soon can be very damaging to your credit.

Try sticking to only one credit card at a time. Establish a good rating with that one and use it for a couple of years before trying to apply for a new one. Your credit rating will remain strong if you don't race out of the gate but start building it up slow and steadily.

4. Pay Your Balance in Full Every Month

You've probably heard that it's important to pay your balance in full every month. If you are only charging what you can afford to pay, this is not a problem. When you are careful with your spending and can pay off your balance each month, you show your creditors that you are responsible. As a result, you'll end up with a higher credit score.

5. Pay on Time

One of the most important things you can do when it comes to paying your bills is to *pay on time*. It is important to make it a habit to pay everything on time so that it doesn't have a chance to negatively affect your score. Any bill that has the possibility of becoming delinquent and end up being sent to a collection agency can harm your credit.

6. Manage Balances Properly

There will be times when you have to carry a balance on some big-ticket items. If you find that you can't pay the balance in full at the end of the month, make sure that you pay a significant amount so that you are paying more than interest payments on the debt owed.

Always try to pay more than the minimum payment each month until you pay your balance down. When you do that and keep your balance owed to less than 30% of your credit limit, you protect your credit and can maintain a relatively high score.

7. **Allow Your Accounts to Mature**

Having good credit can be a good thing, but the longer you have it, the better. As your accounts mature it looks good on a credit report. When you keep the oldest accounts active, they give your credit image a boost. Keep in mind that if you close any account, it may take several years before it drops off of your record, so leave them open, even if you don't plan to use them. This will show creditors that you are not relying on it to get by.

Establishing good credit is extremely important for anyone who is seeking financial freedom. While there are several ways to reach that goal, establishing a good budget, and sticking to it is a surefire key to success. But budgeting doesn't have to mean months of drudgery and deprivation as some people have been led to believe. If you do it the right way, find a plan that works well with your lifestyle and personality, you're well on your way to discovering the freedom that comes from managing your money well.

It's not enough to have a good budget; you need to know how to implement it properly. That includes knowing how to use credit wisely. Setting up a good financial future, should not feel like a punishment, but should feel uplifting and rewarding. By following these very basic guidelines you can find success along the way and the big pay-off years down the line.

Chapter 3: Investing 101

Learning how to manage your money is a big step towards gaining financial freedom, but once you've succeeded, you're only half-way there. The reality is that finding wealth and financial security rarely comes from good management of credit and savings accounts.

Those two features can put you in a better financial position, but they don't erase the fact that you still need to work for your money. A savvy financial planner understands that the transition from working for your money to having your money work for you is a huge step. To get your money to work for you means that you have to invest.

Types of Investments to Add to Your Portfolio

There are a wide variety of investment options available for anyone who is willing to take the risk. Understanding your level of risk tolerance can make a major difference in which investment tools you choose to make. When making investment decisions, you need to decide if you're willing to invest for the long haul or you want a quick return and make a short-term investment. For most people, the first line of investment options for the long-term are either in stocks or bonds, but there's a wide variety of options to choose from.

1. **Stocks**

Financial Freedom Investing

In its most basic definition, a stock is a purchase of a small portion of a specific company. When you buy a share, you are actually buying a percentage of the business' potential earnings and assets. When a business sells shares in its company, it is doing so in order to raise capital to invest in its own operations. As an investor, you can buy or sell your shares to improve your own financial portfolio.

When the value of the stock increases, an investor can then sell his shares at a higher price than what he bought it for and make a profit. Another way to make money in stocks is by purchasing stocks that pay dividends. Dividends are distributions of earnings given out periodically to investors. You can choose to invest in dividend stocks or growth stocks.

With dividend stocks, you will receive a regular distribution of earnings without the need to sell your interest in the business. Dividends can be paid out monthly, quarterly, bi-annually, annually or on some other payment schedule. Most companies that pay out dividends are pretty well-established and in most cases are considered safe.

Growth stocks are also shares in companies that are expected to see a certain amount of growth. They don't pay out any dividends, so you don't get a regular payout for owning them. The only way to turn a profit with a growth stock is to sell your shares in the business.

There is a certain level of risk with both options. Dividend stocks are usually the preferred choice for those with a low-risk tolerance.

Growth stocks are a little less predictable but that doesn't mean they are less stable. There are times when the profits from a growth stock can actually be more rewarding than dividends.

If you're thinking of investing in the stock market, it just makes sense for you to compare the two, learn your level of risk tolerance, and decide which type works best for you.

2. Bonds

When you purchase a bond, you are technically lending money to the issuer and will receive a certain amount of interest for allowing them access to your funds.

For the most part, bonds are believed to be much safer than stocks, but the possibilities for grand returns is rare. You also have an additional risk to worry about. Just like with any company that extends loans to others, there is always a risk of the borrower going into default. Government bonds are usually safer because they are backed by the "full faith and credit" of the United States federal government. Next to government bonds in safety are state and city bonds. Corporate bonds come with more risk but are considered to be the third safest choice.

Investors earn profit from regular interest payments from the borrower, which is usually paid once or twice each year with the principal being paid back on the maturity date. Bonds are fixed-income investments, which means the amount of the investment is fixed and does not change.

3. Mutual Funds

When you purchase a mutual fund, you are investing in a larger number of stocks with one single transaction. The funds collect money from a wide range of investors and then invest that money into select stocks, bonds, or assets.

These investment instruments are found and selected based on a set strategy. For example, one fund may only be a specific type of stocks or bonds, while others may have a different set of parameters. One fund may choose to work only with international stocks while another may want to focus on technology or the sciences.

Profits are made when the selected list of investments goes up in price. The money received could be in the form of dividends or interest. Periodically these are dispersed to the customer. Also, when the investments actually do increase in value, owners are free to sell their interest for a profit.

4. Index Funds

An index fund is one type of mutual fund which passively tracks all the stocks in a particular index. This type of fund doesn't use a fund manager to choose which stocks to invest in. Rather, the decision is based on all the stocks in that particular index. For example, one well-known index fund is the Standard & Poor's 500, which has the goal of matching the performance of the S&P 500 by holding shares in every one of the companies listed in that index.

One of the biggest advantages of investing in index funds is their low cost. Because there is no need to have a live person to manage the fund, you save money.

Index funds earn money through either dividend or interest payments made periodically. They can also make money when the value of their investment increases. Investors can sell their share in the fund when the price goes up.

5. Exchange Traded Funds (ETFs)

One type of index fund is an exchange-traded fund or an ETF. ETFs strive to copy the performance of a specific kind of index. Because they are also not actively managed, they are also much cheaper than mutual funds.

You can purchase ETFs on the regular stock exchange and sell them the same way. The price will fluctuate up and down throughout the day, just like regular stocks. However, both mutual and index funds have a fixed price that is only adjusted at the end of each trading day.

Profits are earned the same as with all other funds. Some ETFs pay dividends or interest rates, but you can also make money when the fund increases in value and you sell it at a profit.

6. Options

An option is simply a contract to buy or sell a particular stock at a pre-determined price or on a set date. Even though you enter into a contract, you are not required to buy or sell the stock, so you have the flexibility to decline the offer if you choose to. The contract only gives you an "option" to make such a transaction. You also have the option to sell the contract to another investor or let it expire.

An options contract allows you to lock in a particular stock at a lower price. If you are right, you are opting in on a chance to purchase the stock at a later date at a more favorable price than the rest of the market. If your predictions are wrong, you lose only the money you invested in buying the contract and walk away.

You will have to open a brokerage account with either your bank or an investment firm. Once the account is opened and funded, you can start making your investment.

However, you have to be very careful with the fees. Some firms will charge monthly fees while others will charge for every transaction. When calculating your profits, make sure that once you've made your decision, the profits you claim are not eaten up by the costs of making that transaction.

Understanding the Bond Market

Before you purchase a bond, you need to do a little research. There are loads of online resources that will help you to find the best bonds to invest in. Look for sites that will break down all of the information on the different securities, any news related to their performance, analysis, and other vital information that can help you to make a decision. Some of the most frequently used sites include Investopedia, Morningstar, Yahoo, and the Finance Bond Center.

As an individual investor, you cannot personally invest in the bond market. You will have to enlist the aid of an institutional investor. Most do this through their employee pension fund, their banks, an endowment fund, or an investment banker. If you don't have any one of these at your disposal, your next step would be to find an asset manager to make the investment for you.

There are three groups that are active in the bond market.

Issuers: Those that develop, register, and/or sell bonds on the market. These could be corporations or they could be from a governmental agency. We are probably most familiar with US Treasury bonds, which are issued by the Treasury Department, but there are other agencies that also issue bonds. Most bonds issued from the government will reach maturity after 10 years.

Underwriters: A group that evaluates the risks of each of the bonds. They buy securities from the issuers and then resells them to the buyers for a profit.

Participants: Participants buy bonds as loans to the various entities. The loans are extended for the length of the security and receive the face value of the bond once it reaches its maturity date.

Grades are issued by a bond rating agency and usually come in the form of a letter grade. For example, a "AAA" rating is considered very high quality and is least likely to go into default. A "BBB" rating is considered to be a medium risk, and anything that is a BB or lower is considered a high-risk investment opportunity.

Understanding the Stock Market

The stock market is where you buy shares in publicly traded companies. Like bonds, there are different types of stocks: common stocks, options, and futures.

The primary role of the stock market is to bring buyers and sellers together in a controlled environment. The market ensures that all securities are traded fairly, honestly, and with transparency. They keep trade between investors and corporations above board.

The stock market has two separate components. The first is set aside for new businesses offering initial public offerings or IPOs for trade. Underwriters set the initial price of securities for sale. IPOs tend to be higher risk investments as most of these corporations have not yet proven their worth.

The second component is for trading equities for the more established businesses. This is where the majority of trading on the stock market takes place.

There are several different stock exchanges, each one offering different securities to trade.

Nasdaq: This is an online electronic exchange that lists the securities issued from companies with a smaller capitalization. Stocks on the Nasdaq includes companies trading in a wide range of industries, including consumer goods, services, utilities, healthcare, and technology.

New York Stock Exchange: The NYSE trades some of the oldest and largest public companies in existence. You have probably heard of the Dow Jones Industrial Average (DJIA), which consists of the top 30 largest companies on the NYSE. These are also the oldest and most referred to indexes in the world.

American Stock Exchange: Initially, it was used for trading completely new asset classes. Today, it is the exchange used for buying and selling ETFs.

There are several distinct differences between the bond market and the stock market. The stock market has a central place of trade where investors of all sorts can buy and sell their interests, where the bond market does not. Also, there is a difference in risk levels between the two. Those who choose to invest in the stock market are likely exposed to a higher level of risk than those who invest in the bond market.

Bonds, however, are more likely to be affected by inflation and interest rates. When there is an increase in interest rates, the prices of bonds tend to drop. On the other hand, if the interest rates are high, the value of the bond itself can be deflated.

Credit risks are also something you need to carefully consider. Purchasing a bond from a company with a poor credit leaves you open to a potential default. In most cases, the issuer may not even be able to make the minimum interest payments on your investment and you could lose a lot more.

Some of the safest investment options to start with are US Treasury bonds. You are less likely to experience a default, but that doesn't mean they are 100% risk-free. They are still susceptible to price volatility over the life of the loan.

Tips on Choosing the Right Stocks for You

Your choice of stocks to trade will depend on several factors. 1) your experience, 2) how much you have to invest, 3) and your actual investment strategy.

Financial Freedom Investing

There are several strategies to consider: day trading, position trading or long-term trading. It is important to note that your trading plan is not a fixed strategy, as it needs to be dynamic and flexible enough to adapt to a constantly changing marketplace. Later, as you begin trading and observing your successes and failures, you'll become wiser in your decisions, recognize your strengths and weaknesses and learn to utilize that new knowledge more effectively.

Before you begin:

1. Know your goals. What do you hope to accomplish with your financial portfolio? Those who are looking to generate an income will look at low-growth firms in stable industries like utilities, REITs (Real Estate Investment Trusts), and partnerships. If you have a clear picture of your risk tolerance and how you will manage it, you will be looking to preserve your capital by investing in premium blue-chip stocks.

2. If you're more interested in preserving capital, then you might focus your attention on those companies that go through various life cycle stages and ranging market caps.

3. All stocks will go up and down in price, but they won't all rise at the same time. By investing in a wider range of stocks, you'll have a better chance of generating a consistent amount of income with no significant downsides to deal with.

4. Be observant. When investing in stocks, you are always learning. Stay up to date on all current market events. Make it a habit to read blogs, study magazines, and keep abreast of the latest financial news. You should do this on a daily basis.

5. Finding the right company. Start by tracking the performance of a chosen industry and then look at the stocks listed in that industry. Check out the ETF for the industry and see what companies they are holding.

6. Filtering by sector or industry can be a good start, but you can expand the search even further and filter your list by other details like market cap, dividend yield, or other practical metrics that will help you to decide.

7. Don't waste your energy on trying to catch the absolute bottom of any stock price, nor should you try to stay in a trade until it maxes out at the very top. Keep your focus on growing your net worth and get out when you know it will be to your benefit.

8. Don't give in to FOMO, or the fear of missing out. View each trade as a learning experience and tap into the ones you can and forget about the ones you can't.

9. Choose only one stock to begin with and study the results over time.

10. Use trading charts to give you a clear understanding of the market and stock movements.

11. Follow through with your plan until you get the desired results.

Choosing Stocks That Fit Your Personality

We are naturally drawn to those things that we understand the best. If you are a young twenty-something and have spent your formative years playing lots of video games, you have a quick mind, and know how to stay focused, short-term investing may be the best strategy for you.

On the other hand, if you're nearing retirement age, are slow at making decisions, and like to look at things from all angles, then maybe day trading would be a better choice. If your goal is to generate a little extra income from one month to the next, then dividend trading might be your best option.

Whatever investment style you choose, think it through carefully. It is very important that you understand the stock's volatility, price movements, and expected performance.

Manage Your Risk

Every investment option comes with its own level of risk. Your goal is to preserve your capital and manage that risk with every decision you make. Even if you suffer losses, you want to be sure that you have enough capital left to keep something in play.

Every investment you choose should be an educational experience. Take the time to analyze and calculate the costs, striving to make an informed decision.

Financial Freedom Investing

Don't Over Complicate It

Keep it as simple as possible. Every stock has its own set of habits and moves; the more you understand these habits — the easier it will be to anticipate how it moves and make decisions accordingly. Once you feel comfortable with one stock, add another, and repeat the process. If you continue this pattern, you are less likely to find yourself in over your head.

What Is an Investment Plan?

Basically, it is a plan of how you will invest in the stock market. It dictates your actions so you don't make impulse decisions that can put your capital at risk. Here is a sample Day Trading plan you can start with until you get your feet wet:

1. Trade one stock at a time
2. When I am familiar with that stock, I will invest in a second one.
3. Trade only within the $20–$40 price range
4. Trade stocks that have an average 30-day volume that ranges a minimum of 1 million shares and a maximum of 2 million
5. The stock should have a medium degree of volatility
6. No trading in biotech stocks
7. I will max my portfolio at five stocks
8. I will study each of the stock's performance during multiple time frames every night
9. I will follow S&P Futures

Financial Freedom Investing

Here is a sample plan for swing trading

1. Select up to 50 stocks for trade
2. Invest in one at a time
3. When I am comfortable and familiar with one then I will add another
4. The price will be $25 or more
5. Stocks will have an average 30-day volume of 500,000 shares a day or more
6. I will choose 25 for a long watch list

    a. Each will have increasing revenues and earnings
    b. They will have high relative strength in its leading sectors
    c. They will be above the 200 moving average
    d. They should be following the S&P Futures

7. I will choose 25 for my short watch list

    a. These will have declining revenues and earnings
    b. They will have a low relative strength in the leading sectors
    c. They will perform below the 200 moving average
    d. They should be following the S&P Futures

8. I will study the stochastics signal

The 5 Best Stock Trading Strategies of All Time

Financial Freedom Investing

Once you've decided on the company to invest in, you're probably eager to get started making money. You need a strategy that dictates just how you want to invest. There are five different strategies for investing in stocks, and it pays to understand a little about each of them to help you determine how you will invest your money.

General Trading: You are anticipating the moves of the overall market, looking for averages that will give you an idea of their direction.

Selective Trading: Selective trading means you will pick out stocks which you expect to perform better than the overall market over the course of the next year.

Buy Low Sell High: Enter the market when the prices are at an extreme low. If you choose well and the stock recovers, you can make a pretty tidy little profit.

Long-Pull Selection: Choose the businesses you expect to prosper over the long-term and will fare better than the average business within their industry.

Bargain Purchases: Choosing stocks that you know are selling below their market value.

Your approach to investing should not be based on impulses but should be thought out rationally, then applied with deliberate discipline. This way, you won't find yourself fretting over every change you see in the market but will be comfortable with your decisions and can understand the movements when they happen.

8 Worst Investing Mistakes to Avoid

When you do things deliberately, you're protecting yourself and your finances. However, new investors often give in to the powerful urge to take a chance on that one risky investment. That and several other mistakes are often at the heart of major financial losses in the market. Learning to avoid these can make a huge difference in how fast you build your portfolio and put you on the right track towards greater profits.

1. ***Investing Before You Understand.*** If you are not well-versed in one industry, you should avoid those stocks. Endeavor to understand the business model and how it plans to increase its profits. Always strive to get a clear picture of where the business is going and how it plans to get there before you commit.

2. ***Allowing Your Love of a Company Overshadow Good Judgment.*** Sometimes we fall in love with a company that is doing very well on the market. Never forget your goal is not to support a company that you love but to make money. While the stock may be doing well, its fundamentals can change at any time, so always keep abreast of what's happening with your stock and events that could impact it. Never love a stock so much that you can't sell it.

3. ***Failing to Exercise Patience.*** It is always wise to exercise patience when investing; the slow, deliberate movement often pays off better than those fast bursts to the top. Your expectations should be realistic so that you're not discouraged when things don't happen quickly.

4. ***Jumping in and Out of Trades too Often.*** While you may make a profit here and there, frequent trades incur frequent fees that will usually eat up any profits you make. Add to that the taxes you will have to pay later, and you could easily end up losing a boatload of money rather than boosting your bottom line.

5. ***Trying to Time the Market.*** Your chances are more likely to meet success from making informed decisions rather than trying to hit the market at a specific time.

6. ***Trying to Get Even.*** If you experience a loss in the market, it is best to walk away rather than wait for an opportunity to regain your money. Holding onto the stock could see you losing even more money as the price continues to slide. It is better to preserve at least some of your investment by selling your position and reinvesting what's left in a more stable option.

7. ***Not Diversifying.*** Always invest in more than one industry. This spreads your exposure over a wide range of possibilities and protects your assets. Try to allocate funds to all major sectors and avoid spending more than 10% of your portfolio into one single asset.

8. *Making Emotional Decisions.* Keep a cool head and let your logic govern your decisions. Keep your focus on the long-term results and the averages. It will keep you sane in this business and prevent you from making hasty decisions that could cost you in the long-run.

9. **Create an Action Plan.** Never try to beat the market, but always work towards your personal goals. Be realistic about your expectations and avoid jumping into a stock that makes promises that you know are too good to be true.

10. **Make Your Plan Automatic.** Once you put your plan into action, keep adding to it. Building your investment should continue on throughout your life.

11. **Take Advantage of Your Profits.** There is nothing wrong with skimming a little of your money off the top to enjoy right now, today. Perhaps at the end of the year, you can take 5% of your profits for a little fun. This will give you the incentive to keep pushing forward towards your goals and growing your portfolio.

No doubt, you will make mistakes when you invest in the stock market. Get used to it. It is a major part of investing. However, you can minimize the number of mistakes you make by following these basic guidelines. They will help you to become a better investor over time. By making decisions based on actual facts and data rather than emotions, you will be one step ahead of every other new investor that enters the market.

Chapter 4: Dividend Stocks

How would it feel if you could have a steady stream of income coming in on a regular basis without having to lift a finger to work? Most of us have dreamed about that happening, but some have actually been able to find it through dividend stocks. When you invest in dividend stocks, you are essentially building an ongoing income that will last as long as the company you invest in remains profitable.

However, before you drop all of your money into these stocks, you need to learn just how the dividend system works. How dividends are paid, and the different types of dividends you can choose. You probably enter this arena knowing that dividends are paid on different stocks but understanding how to find and capitalize on cash dividends, stock dividends, and property dividends can make all the difference in how well your investments perform. Here are some basic tips that will help you to enter this type of investment opportunity without making costly mistakes along the way.

When a Company Pays Dividends

Not all companies that earn a profit pay dividends. Some choose to hold onto their profits and then reinvest them back into the business, either by reducing their debt or expanding their operations. Companies that pay out dividends are literally sharing a percentage of their profits with their shareholders. Those who choose to invest in dividend stocks usually have the ultimate goal of using those regular payments to support themselves.

Before a dividend is paid out, it has to first be approved by the company's Board of Directors. If the company pays out monthly, then they have to have approval every month. Once the dividend is approved, there are three dates that an investor needs to know.

Declaration date: the date the company makes a public announcement of its decision to pay a dividend.

Ex-Dividend date: the date the decision is made as to who will be paid. Any shareholders on record on that date will receive a dividend for each share they own.

Payment date: This is the date the dividend is actually distributed to the shareholders. Most dividends are paid out quarterly, but there are several that pay monthly, bi-annually, or annually as well.

Visiting sites like Dividend.com will tell you how often dividends are paid for each stock and how much. For example, if you see a company is paying out $1.00/share every quarter, it means that investors are receiving $.25/share four times a year, not $1 four times a year.

Different Types of Dividends

The most common form of dividend payments is cash dividends. These are paid directly from the profits generated over a period of time. There are several different types of cash dividends. If you own preferred stock, then the company must make those dividend payments preferred shareholders first, before any payments are paid out to common stockholders. Preferred stock dividends are automatically set but common stock dividends can be changed, suspended, or even stopped completely based on the discretion of the Board of Directors.

1. ***Property Dividends.*** Some companies prefer to give property rather than cash to their shareholders. Property can take any form depending on the holdings of the company. A property dividend could be anything from pencils to gold to cars to salad dressings. These are recorded at market value on the declaration date.

2. ***Special Dividends.*** Occasionally, a company may choose to make a special dividend for various reasons. These are usually one-time distributions that follow a major success in the business. Perhaps they won major litigation in court, they sold a portion of the business, or they successfully liquidated an investment. These special dividends can be either cash, additional shares in the company or property.

3. ***Stock Dividends.*** Stock dividends are when an investor receives additional shares in the company rather than a cash distribution. There are a number of reasons why a company may choose to issue shares this way. They may not have enough cash on hand to pay out a cash dividend, or they are trying to dilute the value of the stock to encourage more investors to begin trading. Lowering the price is an excellent enticement to invest. With more shares in the market, the value per share drops. It is a lot easier for investors to pay for a $10 share than one that's $100.

4. ***Stock Split.*** A stock split is very similar to a stock dividend. A company may opt to double, triple, or quadruple the number of outstanding shares. With a stock split, the value of each share is lowered, but each investor still has the same overall value of his investment. If you owned 100 shares at $100 each and the company offers a 2-1 stock split, you now own 200 shares at $50 each.

Whether or not dividend investing is right for you depends on your goals. When a company decides it is going to pay out dividends, one of the first things it considers is its ability to reinvest the cash it has on hand at a higher rate of interest than the shareholders could. For example, if a company you're investing in is earning 25% on its equity and they have no debt hanging over their head, management could decide to hold all of its earnings confident that the investor will not find another company that is able to bring in that much of a return.

From the investor's perspective, you might be only interested in investing in that company for the dividend to cover your living expenses. These types of investors are not necessarily interested in the actual value of the shares, but in whether or not you're going to be able to pay your bills with the dividends you earn.

The Payout Ratio

The payout ratio is the percentage of net income a company pays out as a dividend. It is important to understand this ratio when choosing which stocks to invest in. This percentage gives you the projected growth of a company and what you can expect from it going forward.

To calculate the payout ratio, look at the company's cash flow statement. For example, if a company's statement says that it paid out $2.166 billion in dividends to shareholders and its income statement says that it had a net income of $4.347 billion, you could calculate the ratio using the following formula.

$2,166,000,000 dividends

$4,347,000,000 net income

The answer 49.8% gives a pretty revealing figure. It shows that the company paid out nearly half of its net profits to shareholders over the year.

The Dividend Yield

Another box you will see when you look up a company's dividend history is the dividend yield. This tells you just how much you are earning in relation to the price of a share of a common stock at the current market price. When you buy a stock that has a high dividend yield, it can generate a nice source of income.

To calculate the dividend yield, divide the annual dividend by the current share price. So, if you were to invest in Starbucks today, your dividend yield would be calculated like this.

$1.44/94.16 = 1.53%

Dividends and Your Taxes

Dividends are taxed at a lower rate than your regular income taxes. Some dividends referred to as "qualified dividends" can be taxed at a higher rate in line with a capital gains tax. To avoid falling into this trap, in order for your dividends earned to be included in that lower rate tax bracket, you must hold the stocks for a minimum of 60 days.

Choosing Stocks That Pay High Dividends

When choosing to invest in dividend stocks, you want to find those that pay the highest of dividends. There are thousands of stocks that pay dividends, so you should be careful to examine each one closely. Look for those companies that have a history of steadily increasing dividends over at least twenty years. Analyze the company's past record until you are confident that they are in a position to continue this trend for the foreseeable future.

Keep in mind that a company's ability to pay dividends is directly related to its cash flow. You are looking for stability. A company can report a net loss and still have a healthy cash flow. If a company is lowering its dividend, you can bet that it's going to lose some stability as investors start to pull out. They will not lower their payout for a problem that they expect to be only temporary. On the other hand, a company that increases its dividend will only do so if the business is capable of maintaining the higher rate for an extended period of time.

DRIPS

As you start to earn dividends, the amount of money you receive may seem miniscule at best, but that's okay. Unless you need a healthy stream of cash flowing in, you can turn around and reinvest that money into buying more stocks through a Dividend Reinvestment Plan (DRIP).

When you enroll in a DRIP plan, you will no longer receive dividend payments, but the money will automatically be used to buy additional shares of the same stock. There are several reasons why you would want to do this:

- The small earnings will automatically be reinvested.
- Most DRIPS plans have minimal or no commission fees
- You are allowed to purchase fractional shares, which over time can increase your wealth significantly.
- You can split your dividend repurchase plan, so you still receive some cash payout while the rest of the money goes to purchase additional shares.

Remember, for every share you purchase, the dividend payout you receive will increase, but with DRIPS, you won't be putting any more of your working capital into the account, and the investment will begin to pay for itself.

Think of how this could work to your benefit. Imagine owning 1,000 shares of a company valued at $49 per share. The annual dividend payout is 1.50/share paid out quarterly. You would receive a quarterly payment of .375 for each share or $375.00. You could receive all of that money each quarter with no problem, but if you don't need the cash to cover living expenses, then you could enroll in DRIPS and reinvest all of it (or some of it) to purchase additional shares of the same stock. $375 could buy you another 7 shares. The next time a dividend payout is due, your income would have moved from $375 to $377.62.

If you continue to repeat this pattern over the next 10 to 20 years, you could see how this would increase your earnings without you ever having to put another dime in the pot. DRIPS is giving yourself a raise.

How to Find the Best Dividend Stocks for Your Portfolio

In order to generate enough of an income from dividends, most people invest in high dividend stocks. When you make good choices and consistently contribute to your portfolio, you can generate quite a passive income that you can live off of during your later years. The most successful investors build up a portfolio based on higher dividend payouts.

There are several ways to find these stocks, but you have to be careful. Often looking at dividend yields can be deceiving, so you need to always be conscious of a possible dividend trap. You need to find those high dividend stocks and still give yourself some type of protection against potential risks where dividends could be cut or eliminated.

- The payout ratio should not exceed 70%, which means that the company is retaining a minimum of 30% of its earning to reinvest.
- Look for companies with a good pricing flexibility. That way, they can raise their prices if the inflation rate becomes too high. This keeps the money flowing into your bank account, even if the economy is not stable.
- Look at the debt-to-equity ratio of the company. It should be 50% or less. This tells you that there is a $1 of net worth to every $1 of debt the company holds.
- The P/E ratio should be 15 or less, which can provide some protection just in case the dividend is cut for some reason.

Do Not Make These 10 Dividend Investing Mistakes

Buying dividend stocks can be tricky. While the potential for profit is great, you can easily fall into huge pitfalls if you're not careful in your search. Don't be hasty in making a decision. Still, with a little knowledge you can avoid many of the mistakes often associated with these kinds of investments.

1. ***Don't Trust a Hot Tip.*** It doesn't matter how much you trust the person giving it, a tip is only a tip. You can trust someone's sincerity but make it a rule to always verify the information you receive. At the very least, you should look up the company's statements over the last year or two and run the numbers yourself. Look under the hood, kick the tires and so on. Check to see if any insiders are buying shares or if possible, talk directly with someone in the company who may know what's in line for the future.

2. ***Do the Work.*** Yes, doing the research can be a real pain, but it will pay off in the end. Always do the homework. This will help to keep you from being too emotionally invested in a potential stock. When you understand what you're buying and know how the company is being managed, you're less likely to make an impulse decision that you might regret later. If the market takes a dive, you will know exactly why and already have a back-up plan to cut your losses.

3. ***Don't Buy/Sell for the Dividend Alone.*** Don't buy the stock just to get the dividend and then sell it right afterward. You'll lose money. Yes, you will collect the dividend as promised, but in most cases, the price of the share will drop considerably after the payout. At the very best, you can expect to break even. Investors rarely make money on this type of trade, and much of what you earn will be eaten up with fees and commissions.

4. ***Look Beyond the Yield.*** Just because a stock has a high yield doesn't always mean that it's not in trouble. Don't be blinded by a high yield to convince you that a stock is worth it. Some companies that have a low yield are far steadier and more reliable than those with a volatile history and a high yield. Always look at the big picture before making a decision. You want to know why the yield is high. Is it because it pays high dividends or because of its low share price?

5. ***Look to the Future.*** When you research a stock, you are looking at either its history or where it stands in the present. This is important because it gives you a real time picture of what you can expect from the company. Your goal is to

generate a passive income that you can rely on in later years so you also need to know what to expect in the future.

If you are smart, you will look at the company's history to see how well it has performed in the past and use that information to project into the future. If they have historically raised dividends periodically in the past, it might be reasonable to believe they will continue that trend, especially if the numbers look good. Keep a watchful eye out for any news that could have an impact on the company's development or other issues that may not be readily apparent.

6. ***Always Keep a Watch on the Market.*** Don't assume that because you've invested in a company that has a solid history, good numbers, and has hit all of your earmarks, that you should just let everything ride. Even the big stable companies will one day come crashing down. Of the thousands of companies that were on the NYSE 100 years ago, less than two dozen remain. That means that even the massive conglomerates of the past have one day crashed and burned. Always keep a close eye on the market. It's the only way to protect your investment.

7. ***Buying a Stock Based Solely on the Price.*** There is a huge difference between a share price and its actual value. You need to understand this difference. Just because a stock has a low price and appears more affordable doesn't guarantee that it's a good deal. Buying based purely on price is not investing, it is merely gambling, which doesn't yield the kind of results you need to build up a portfolio.

8. ***Keeping a Bad Stock for Too Long.*** When a stock is performing poorly, dump it. That stock is not your friend; it's

Financial Freedom Investing

not someone you owe anything to. If the price is plummeting and there is no indication that it is going to recover anytime soon, waiting to sell is almost a guarantee that you're going to lose. Get rid of it, don't let emotions dictate what you should do; there are thousands of other options that will earn you money. If the stock does recover later on, you can always buy back in.

9. **Don't Forget Your Taxes.** Too often, investors get wrapped up in their earnings and fail to account for the debt they owe to Uncle Sam. Anytime you are earning money, there will be taxes to be paid. No matter what investment tool you use, if you're not sure of your tax obligations, talk to a tax accountant and play it safe. You should do this every year, because tax laws change frequently. You will need to adjust your investment plan to ensure that your earnings are more than enough to keep the IRS at bay.

10. **Taking the Media Too Seriously.** When you start to research different stocks there will be an endless stream of media reports, financial analysts, and opinions about what is a good or a bad stock. Many of them have very good information to consider but they are not always right. The value of their information is only as good as their resources. No source is 100% reliable. Always do your best to verify any information you receive, especially if you are not getting it directly from the company itself.

Choosing the best high dividend stocks is not rocket science, but it can make you feel like you're navigating one the craters on the moon. There are so many dark areas where you can get into trouble, you will have to be extra careful not to fall into any of the traps that catch so many novice investors.

What You Need to Know About Dividend Tax Rates

As your profits start to roll in, it is important to keep everything in perspective. As much as you'd like to think so, all of that money is not yours. As usual, Uncle Sam is sitting on the sideline waiting for his share. Once you start collecting dividends, you'll have to set some of those proceeds aside to keep him appeased.

Most dividends are paid in the form of cash but depending on where you decide to put your investments, you may also receive them in the form of additional stocks, stock options, property, services, or options. No matter what instrument you invest in, it is considered profit, and you must claim it on your income taxes.

Ordinary vs. Qualified Dividends

There are two different types of dividends you might be receiving. Ordinary dividends are those received from the profits of a company. The amount you receive is usually based on the type of stock you have. Preferred stocks pay more than the common stock investments, but any dividend received from a preferred stock will still be considered an ordinary dividend unless it is stipulated otherwise.

Qualified dividends meet the IRS's requirements for capital gains taxes, which are taxed at a higher rate than ordinary dividends. Depending on your tax bracket, you could expect to pay anywhere from nothing to as much as 20% of your income.

Under the current tax laws, you must report all dividend income received even if it is only a small amount. If you received more than $10 from any one company, you will need to file a Form 1099-DIV declaring the exact amount you received. If the dividends you received come from a trust, estate or an S-corporation, you should also file a Schedule K-1, which will determine the percentage of dividends that you must pay taxes on.

You should automatically receive the required forms you should file from the company, but if for some reason you don't, you are still required to report the income on your tax return. Even if you don't receive an actual payout of those dividends, the IRS still sees them as taxable income. So, even if you reinvest them into purchasing more stocks, you are still required to report that as income.

How to Report Dividends

You can report your dividend income on your regular 1040 From. If your total income received amounts to more than $1,500 or if some of the dividends you receive are as a nominee for someone else, then you must also file a Schedule B form.

The thrill of seeing your money working for you can be truly amazing, but to ensure that those successes you receive are not dampened by trouble with the IRS, always take the time to file your income properly. This way, you can really enjoy the money you earn without reservation.

" # Chapter 5: Day Trading

If dividend investing is a little too slow for you, a faster way to get generate new cash is with day trading.

What Is Day Trading?

Day trading works the same as regular stock market investing, but all of your transactions are completed within one trading day. In essence, you buy and sell before the close of the trading day. Traders who make these types of trades are considered to be speculators, a form of trading that carries much higher risks.

One of the reasons for closing during a single day is to protect the gains investors might have received throughout the course of the trading day. Once the market closes, events can happen that could reverse the trend and they would be unable to manage things. A drop in prices can easily occur after the close of one day and before the open of the next and with that drop, much of their profits could go with it. However, by selling your position before the close of the day, you lock in whatever profits you have earned and thus cut your risks.

Day trades can be made in any market but are most commonly transacted in the stock or the foreign trade markets. Investors rely heavily on leverage for these short-term trading strategies, focusing on making their money on seemingly insignificant price movements.

Financial Freedom Investing

As a day trader, you will need to keep abreast of any news events that may have an impact on the trades you're making. This strategy is called "trading the news" where you respond to economic statistics, interest rate movements, or corporate earnings. These types of events are subject to market psychology, and investors will react with quick but significant moves. Day traders anticipate these movements and take advantage of them to capitalize on their earnings.

While the risk can be very high, the attraction of day trading is the potential for amazingly fast and impressive profits. To get those though, you need to be a fast decision-maker, disciplined, and diligent enough to do the required research to improve your chances of success.

There are many reasons why you might want to try your hand at day trading.

- You can profit when the price is rising and when it is falling
- You get additional margin and can use the leverage and the quick movements in the market to capitalize on gains.
- While research is necessary, detailed research into a company's fundamentals is not necessary. You are tapping into small fluctuations so you don't need long-term investment strategies.
- You earn cash fast.

These are just some of the advantages of entering into day trading. If you think you have the fortitude and are a fast thinker, then the next step is to just pick a stock and start trading.

How to Start Day Trading

Day trading sounds simple enough, but there is definitely a learning curve. Picking the best stocks to trade is only the beginning. The most successful traders have become very skilled at applying what they call the "The Rule of the Three P's," Planning, Practice, and Patience.

Planning. You will definitely need a trading plan to get started. Develop a personal map to help you navigate your trades. You are entering a highly volatile market and things will be moving quickly. If you're not prepared, you'll miss your marks and end up losing more money than you'll gain.

Practice. You won't get it right the first time out of the gate. It might be best to practice with one of the online trading platforms that let you test out your theories before you actually put money in the game. The more practice you get, the better you'll be at predicting when many of these volatile movements will happen. If you don't get it right, don't let that discourage you. Some of the most experienced day traders miss out from time to time. Just keep trying until you hit your rhythm.

Patience. Once you have a good trading plan and you get started, you'll experience some ups and downs. You need patience enough to stick to your plan to the end.

A day trader knows the when, what, and how to trade every stock before he enters the market. To do that, you need to understand how to use volatility to your advantage.

Volatility is directly linked to the activity of short-term traders and reflects the dispersion of a stock's returns on the market index. It can be determined by the difference between a stock's high and lows for a given day and then divided by the actual price for the same day. But the fluctuation of the price is only one factor that measures volatility. For example, a stock with a $50 share price that fluctuates as much as $5 in a single day is considered to be a lot more volatile than a $150 share that also fluctuates in the $5 range. It is the percentage of the move that also factors into its volatility.

The best day traders look to trade the most volatile stocks. It is the most efficient means of making money fast. These stocks tend to offer the best profit potential, but they come with their own level of risk. If you're aiming to try your hand at one of these, you need two things:

1. Where to find the most volatile stocks to trade
2. How to trade them with technical indicators

The best way to find a volatile stock is to run a stock screen through a platform like stockfetcher.com. These sites use filters to track the most active stocks. For example, you can select stocks that average moves of 5% or greater between opening and closing on each of the last 100 days. You can also filter by stock prices as well.

For a more intensive search, another platform you can use is Finviz.com. Its free version will give you a list of the top gainers and the top losers in the market each day. You also have the option to filter the results further, looking for details on market capitalization, volume, and performance. You can be very specific in the type of filters you use so that you can end up with a list of stocks that meet very exacting parameters.

Nasdaq.com also lists the markets biggest gainers and loser, but their results are not filtered for volatility. Instead, you'll get a list of stocks that have the potential of being volatile. You'll need to manually sift through the list to see which stocks have the possibility of going volatile on a trading day.

Now to the question of how to trade them. When you have chosen your stock and are ready to make a trade, you need to be patient and wait for the precise moment to enter the market. One of the biggest advantages you will have is something called "directional bias." This is when specific indicators will be observed that tell you in which way the price is moving. You must always watch the price action to determine if the price is swinging high or low in comparison to previous waves.

The Stochastic Oscillator. Another useful tool you can use is the stochastic oscillator for predicting volatile stocks. This filters for stocks that may not have a very clear trend. Even when a stock is volatile, it can fall into a range before taking off in either direction. Just one single move can quickly change things, so the best thing to do is to hold off until you get confirmation that a price is going to reverse in one way or another.

In such cases, the price may not have a clear-cut direction, but may simply be moving sideways for a time. The best investment strategy is to wait until the price moves above 80 and then falls again. That's when you sell close to or at the top of its range. You can place your stop directly above the new high and your target at 75% of the total range. So, if the range has a high of $1, place your target at $0.25 over the low.

At the bottom, you can establish a long position if the stochastic falls below 20 and begins to rally above it. Place your stop underneath the new low and your target should go 75% up from the bottom. Again, if the range has a high of $1, the target can be at $0.25 below the high.

With the stochastic oscillator, make your trades when they hit 80 and above for uptrends and 20 or below when they are in a downtrend. You will have to move quickly though. If it is truly in a trend, even a delay of one minute could move the price too far away from your target to make any worthwhile trade.

When you are in a trade, ignore signals that may say contrary to what you believe. Let the trade play through. It will either hit the target or the stop.

Volatile stocks are a great way to earn fast money if you have the stomach for it. If you can successfully identify a trend, you will have access to even greater profits. Just follow the directional bias in order to help you make your decision.

Keep in mind that just because a stock is volatile, doesn't necessarily mean that it will trend. Prices can move back and forth sideways for long periods of time. When you see that stochastic reaches either the 80 or 20 mark and then pulls back, it is an indication of a good opportunity to enter the trade.

Day Trading Strategies

There are no hard and fast secrets to successful day trading. While it can be extremely lucrative, it is full of potholes that could cost you just as much, if not more money than you can make. The secret is to develop a well-thought-out plan that you can follow to the letter. The problem with this is that most newbies do not fully understand the game, nor do they have any idea how to create such a plan. Here are just a few tips that can help you develop a good day trading plan to launch you into the market.

1. ***Never Stop Learning.*** The more knowledge you have, the less likely you will make a costly mistake. When you day trade, you need to be aware of all of the latest news in the market. You want to know anything that could happen that might have an impact on the stocks you're investing in. Never shrink back from doing the extra work, it will pay off in the end. This is even more important when the news is directly related to stocks, you're planning on investing in.

2. ***Have an Investment Fund Ready.*** Know exactly how much money you are willing and able to put at risk for every trade you plan to make. On average, day traders usually put up approximately 1-2% of their portfolio into day trades. Some only a half percent. Once you know that amount, portion it out to the stocks you're willing to invest in, but know that there is always a risk, so never put up more than you can lose.

3. ***Make Sure You Have Time.*** Day trading takes time. Because you will have to constantly be watching the movements of the market, it could consume an entire day. If you don't have the time to dedicate to the process, it is better for you to find other ways to invest your money.

4. ***Start Small.*** Don't try to tackle too many stocks at once. When you're beginning, you need to get the feel for the market. Start with only one stock and when you gain your confidence increase it to two. Some even start smaller than that with buying fractional shares rather than a whole single share. Some brokers like Stockpile, will allow you to buy a small percentage of a share, so you can invest in higher-priced stocks without putting a whole lot of money at risk.

5. ***Stay Away From Penny Stocks.*** The tendency for newcomers is to look at the cheapest stocks on the market. Penny stocks are those stocks that are usually priced at $5 or less per share. On the surface, this looks like a great stock to start with, but penny stocks are questionable at best. The chances of getting a windfall from them is minimal. Most stocks that are trading below $5 a share have often fallen to the Penny Stock list because they have been delisted from the major stock exchanges and are already in trouble. Unless you see very clear signs of a reversal, your best bet is to stay clear of these seemingly good bargains.

6. ***Timing is Everything.*** Learn the timing of the market so you know when it's time to jump in. For example, many investors may place an order overnight for the next business day. This means that as soon as the market opens, those orders will be executed so you will see a lot of movement during the first

Financial Freedom Investing

hours of trading, but that is not always a clear picture of market movement. It might be best to wait an extra half an hour until all those orders settle down Usually, the middle of the day is the less volatile with activity increasing the closer you get to the closing bell.

7. ***Take Advantage of Limit Orders.*** Market orders are placed at the best price offered at that specific time. They are not necessarily the best price for you. Limit orders, however, guarantee that the order will only be fulfilled at the price you set. If the price you set is not available, the order will not be filled. Limit orders give you the opportunity to place an order and know exactly the price you will pay.

8. ***Be Realistic.*** No one will win all of the time, but that doesn't mean you can't turn a profit. Your goal is to make more money than you lose. If you keep your limits within a set percentage of your account and plan your entry and exits accordingly, then you have a good chance of gaining more profits than losses, but you will have to stick to your plan and follow through on it.

9. ***Never Lose Your Cool.*** There will be those days when you won't have any idea what the market is doing. On those days, keep your emotions at bay. Always make decisions based on clear logic and reasoning, even if the market is not making any sense at the moment.

10. ***Never Stray From Your Plan.*** When you are day trading, decisions have to be made fast. That can be very difficult if you haven't done your homework. The price could catapult completely out of your reach while you're trying to figure

things out. That's why it's so important to do your homework before you enter the market, so you know the exact point to enter and exit. Creating a plan beforehand and relying on it as a guide is the secret to successful day trade. No matter what the numbers say, don't allow them to lure you into chasing profits but make sure that you follow the day trader's mantra – *Plan your trade and trade your plan.*

Making a Decision

Now that you have made a list of those stocks that are potential winners, you now have to decide which one to buy. A day trader usually looks at three factors:

- **Liquidity.** When a stock is liquid, you have room to enter and exit at a good price. Look for tight spreads between the bid and the asking price, or a low slippage price. The difference between what one would expect to pay for a stock and its actual price.

- **Volatility.** the expected price range within a single trading day. The more volatile the price the greater the chance for profits (or losses).

- **Volume.** How many times a particular stock has been bought and sold within a set time period. When you see a volume increase in a stock, there is heightened interest, and you can expect some type of price jump.

Financial Freedom Investing

Once you've decided what stocks to buy and your plan is set on when to enter the market, you need to decide when to sell. Ideally, you want to sell when the price hits your target, but that is not the only time you can exit.

- Scalping: selling as soon as you make a profit.
- Fading: selling after the price has made a rapid move upward.
- Pivots: selling at the highest price point of the day
- Momentum: selling after news releases or trending moves.

If you find that the interest in the stock is beginning to diminish, you should not hesitate to sell. You should give the same attention to exiting your trade as you do for entering it. Remember, it must be specific enough that you know when to execute it without much deliberating.

Charts

Another way you can determine when to enter the market is by reading chart patterns. Candlestick patterns can take up a whole book on their own. They provide a wealth of ways to look for an entry point. However, one of the most common is the doji reversal pattern.

1. Find a volume spike, which shows if traders are supporting this price level.
2. Find the support for that price. It could be the low or the high of the previous day.
3. Find the level 2 situation, which shows all open orders for that stock.

By following these basic steps, you should be able to anticipate when a price will turn around and offer more favorable positions.

Stop-Loss Orders

Stop-loss orders are meant to manage your losses. The order can be placed either in a low position or above a recent high to automatically sell when the price reaches that point. Using this will protect you from losing everything if the trade doesn't go your way.

Day trading is tricky at best. It is not something that you can get into blindly and expect to win. It takes skill, insight, and discipline. In time, with enough practice and determination, there is a very good chance that you will be successful.

Chapter 6: Real Estate Investing

Real estate opens a wealth of opportunities that one can parlay into a great fortune with the right tools. Unlike investing in the stock market, the principles behind real estate are pretty straightforward. But that doesn't mean that it will be easy breezy when you try to put them into action.

There are three ways you can make money from real estate.

- Increasing property value
- Rentals
- Investing in businesses that depend on real estate

In fact, the three options listed above are the most common ways to generate a nice passive income from the property you own. By learning just a few basic strategies to implement these, you could be well on your way to financial freedom.

Increasing Your Property Value

No matter what you do with your property, outside influences can still have a negative impact on its worth. Every decade or so, there seem to be occasions when the rate of inflation is expected to extend beyond the rate of long-term debt at the time. When that happens, you will find more people willing to extend themselves by borrowing money to finance a major property purchase. Then they sit back and wait for the inflation rate to go back up again. When it does, they can pay off their mortgage with a lower dollar value.

The key is to time the market just right. You need to know how to look at a project, analyze its price and timing, and decide if you will be able to create a good income that will be sufficient enough to support a higher valuation than what is currently evident.

Making Money From Rental Property

While rental property is not always as passive as it might seem, collecting rent is so simple anyone can do it. If you own any kind of property, you can simply rent it out to anyone who wishes to use it. It doesn't even matter what type of property it is; it could be a house, an apartment, or farmland. The money you get from their use of it can be quite lucrative.

As the owner of the property, it will be your responsibility to make sure that the property is being maintained in a usable condition. That means that you will have to be ever vigilant in repairs, supervision, and handling the negative aspects of undesirable tenants. You'll have to be insured against theft or other hazards and be proactive about possible concerns that may come up in relation to your property.

The good news though is that if you are a savvy property owner, there are ways to manage all of those things and still make a tidy profit. There are tools that have been designed that can make property management much easier than it has been in years. One you will find

Financial Freedom Investing

very practical is a special financial ratio, the capitalization rate. To understand this rate and how it works, consider this situation.

If you own a property that is earning $100,00/year and its price is set at $1,000,000, you could apply this formula by dividing the earnings by the value of the house to get the capitalization rate.

$100,000 / $1,000,000 = 0.1 or 10%

You could immediately earn 10% on your investment if you chose to pay cash for the purchase.

You can think of this in the same way you think of stocks. The worth of any real estate property is based on the net present value of the cash it generates for the owner and the cash flow it generates in relation to the price paid for its purchase. In essence, rental income can become a hedge to protect you during economic and financial collapses.

Of course, not all real estate is the same; some will be better suited for generating rental income while others are not. When you make a purchase at the right price but also at the right time, and you can find the right tenant to fill the space, you need not fear any upcoming real estate collapse. You will be collecting a steady stream of rental checks that will carry you through. However, if you don't plan the whole thing right, you could find yourself collecting rents that are far below the market and be stuck in that drain until the market recovers.

Investing in Businesses That Depend on Real Estate

There are lots of businesses that rely heavily on real estate. Many of them, like hotels, provide special services to the public. Other property owners provide office space for businesses, and there are those that can take an empty field and provide useful parking garages for those who drive to the area. Car washes, vending machines, agriculture, and more, the list is endless.

The trick for entering this highly lucrative market is to learn just enough to get started, but not so much that you become overwhelmed. Most new investors learn through a trial-and-error process. In this process, they usually make costly mistakes that can lead them to regrets. However, a plan that will help you to avoid such missteps and get you on the path to passive income can save you a world of time and frustration.

Start Investing One Step at a Time

The steps listed below will help you to make your first initial steps in the real estate market. After you are confident you can carry them out, use them as a checklist to make sure that you don't miss anything crucial that could cost you later on.

Identify Where You Are Financially

Real estate is probably the fastest way to reach financial independence. It is usually the goal that everyone strives to reach. It is one of the best ways to generate enough income to support you financially. But to get to that point, you have to be in a good financial position; you need enough savings to start the ball rolling.

If after looking at your financial situation, you're not quite there yet, there are things you can do to get you there faster.

There are five fundamental stages of wealth:

Stage 1: Survival state – where you are just making enough money to get by. This is the stage where you begin to pay off your debts and get relief from your financial burdens.

Stage 2: Stability state – your finances are not getting worse and you're managing to get your bills paid, and what little you have left you can start saving.

Stage 3: Saver state – you can pay all your bills and have a little bit left over to build up a nice little nest egg.

Stage 4: Growth state – At this point, your savings is turning into a tidy sum that you can seriously consider investing. Your savings should now be generating enough interest that it's worth noticing. If you're reinvesting those earnings, you are starting to get your money to work for you.

Stage 5: Income – you are now in a position where the money you have set aside can generate income for you.

It is important to understand your financial position. Some real estate strategies we discuss later on will be more appropriate for certain stages than others.

Choose Your Investment Strategy

While real estate investing is pretty simple, you still need a business plan. It doesn't have to be detailed, but you need to have a clear idea of what you're going to do. Choose one single strategy that will help you move from the stage you are starting with to the next level. Make sure you build some flexibility into your plan so that you're not derailed by unexpected events. Here are just a few ideas to get your started.

- Lease a large home and sublet rooms to tenants to cover your expenses
- Offer to find good deals for other real estate investors for a fee
- Help buyers find property to invest in, learning the ins and outs of real estate in the process.
- Help landlords find good tenants for their empty spaces
- Become a building manager/superintendent for other real estate investors

These strategies work well for those who are in either the **survival or stability state**. Any of these strategies will allow you to generate extra income without having to shell out a large sum of cash in the process. At the same time, you'll learn everything about the industry without

Financial Freedom Investing

having to spend any extra time taking classes or studying up on the latest policies. It'll be like getting paid to learn.

Start Cutting Back on Your Expenses

If you're at the **saver** stage, then you can do all of the things in the previous stages, but you can also add a few more steps to the process. For one thing, you should start cutting down on your household expenses.

- Use the additional income to pay down your mortgage so you can eliminate your monthly payment.

- Flip your house while you live in it. When you sell it, you create tax-free savings that you can use to invest in other properties.

- Purchase a house that needs significant repairs, move-in while fixing it and then rent it out at a higher price later.

- Become a real estate wholesaler, which is basically collecting a finder's fee for matching the deal with the right investor. This works great for those who may be interested in flipping a house in poor condition or plans to use it for some other profitable purchase. Homeowners who are in jeopardy of foreclosure are more likely to be favorable to such a deal because it allows them to get out from under without having to lose everything.

Financial Freedom Investing

If you are at the **growth** stage, you are ready to grow your net worth into something much bigger. This is the perfect stage for jumping into real estate. There are several ways you can do this:

- Flipping houses: this allows you to generate larger sums of cash to reinvest in other profits.

- Use your savings to pay all cash for property.

- Borrow from several different properties you already own and then pay them down quickly one at a time.

- Buy three properties but sell or rent two. The money from the rental can pay for your living expenses on the third.

- Do a property exchange. Under the IRS's tax-free property exchange you can use Form 1031 to put off paying taxes on any property you sell if you can replace it with a similar piece of property. It makes it possible for you to start small and then grow your portfolio without having to face the negative impact of paying federal taxes with each property you purchase. The process would look like this:

    o You need enough cash on hand for a down payment and closing costs
    o Buy a basic rental property
    o Rent the property and save a portion of the rental for a few years
    o Sell the property

- Use the 1031 form to purchase another, larger property at a discount
- Repeat

Use Your Retirement Account to Purchase Rental Property

By using your tax-free retirement accounts to invest in real estate, you can garner a lot more income to invest, and avoid paying hefty income taxes for your purchase. Self-directed accounts like IRAs, ROTH IRAs, 401Ks allow you to invest those funds in real estate and defer the income taxes you would have otherwise paid.

Maximize Your Income by Utilizing Existing Equity in Your Investments

If you're already at the income stage, you can maximize the income you're generating by selling low-quality properties and buying better ones. You could refinance any of your existing debt and exchange it for fixed low-interest loans and save even more money.

These are just some suggestions for real estate investment strategies. Probably one of them will be more appealing to you than others. Perhaps you have ideas of your own that you would like to consider. The main point is that you have to start with a viable and workable plan to make a success in real estate.

How to Select a Target Market

Your next step would be to pick a target market. Whatever market you choose will have a direct impact on the kind of cash you can generate. Most people prefer to choose a market that is close to their home. It is more efficient and less stressful than investing in properties that are out of your physical reach.

This does not mean that you can't invest in properties far away; it is definitely possible, but you do need to weigh the costs. Whatever market you choose, you need to evaluate the potential carefully.

You also need to do a good market analysis of the area you're interested in. Study the region for employment opportunities, rent prices, and potential population growth. Check the area for the following:

- Is the area convenient?
- Walkability
- Crime
- Schools
- Public transportation
- Local laws
- Taxes
- HOAs
- Etc.

With the above criteria, you can determine if you will be able to work with your target market or if you need to find another location. Start your examination with the larger metropolitan area and then gradually narrow the research down to smaller areas to determine the best location.

1. *Identify Your Criteria for Investment Property*

Determine what you think is a good investment. Write yourself an investment profile that you can show to others. This could be used to generate possible leads to properties you may want to pursue. This list could include property locations, prices, or a specific niche.

Your profile should also have a projection for how much rent you can charge for a property. You might want to start with a basic property to get your feet wet. Choose something you can live in for the moment and then grow from there.

You can find the best land, the most perfect home, at the ideal price, but if it's in a poor location, you may not be able to resell/rent it or if you do, you may not be able to get much of a profit from it.

When you find what you're looking for, even if everything appears to be right, do a little research and check nearby listings in the area. You'll get a pretty good picture of what similar properties are selling for so you can make accurate projections about your potential profits.

Even if you know you're buying a fixer-upper, it is important to have the property inspected. Don't hesitate to ask questions. You need to know how much you're going to need to put into the property and still be able to turn a profit.

Finally, make sure that there is a good chance of turning a profit before you take action. Don't forget to calculate the mortgage rate, utilities, taxes, insurance, repairs, and upkeep. All of that will have a bearing on how successful you'll be with your first investment.

No matter what you do, if the deal doesn't feel right, don't be afraid to walk away. Holding out for the best deals is going to be one of your best secrets to success.

2. *Get Your Support System in Place*

Real estate is best enjoyed with others. While you may be the sole investor on a project, you will still need a team of experts to turn to. Contractors, designers, real estate agents, and advisors could just be the beginning of your list. A good team could be ready to pick up the slack when you get into an area where you lack knowledge and expertise.

3. *Set Up Your Financing Options*

Depending on your credit rating and your financial situation, your options can vary. Here are just a few resources you can tap into.

- Federal Housing Administration
- Veterans Administration
- Conforming Loans (Fannie Mae/Freddie Mac)
- Bank Loans
- Hard Money Loans
- Private Lenders
- Seller Financing

It can be tricky to choose the right lender, but this is where you can call on the advice from your team.

4. *Get Your Down Payment and Closing Costs Ready*

While you can launch your new business with other people's money, you need to have some money of your own to invest. In most cases, a down payment is required to even get the ball rolling. Some down payments can be as little as 3% of the purchase price. Closing costs can also vary. Even in the best of deals, you may need as much as $20,000 of your own cash on hand.

5. *Start Looking for Deals*

Finding the right property requires a lot of legwork. Good deals will not just mysteriously find their way to you, you're going to have to start looking under every rock and peering into every nook and cranny before you find the property that you know is right.

Your marketing budget can be launched with practically nothing, but if you have some money to put towards it, the process gets a lot easier. Here are just a few ideas that have proven to be effective marketing campaigns.

- ***Free campaign:*** Find an agent who will agree to send you leads based on your list of expectations.

- ***Referrals and Networking:*** For a little extra money, you can have business cards or flyers printed with your requirements so that people can contact you when they find something.

- ***Do a Drive or Walk By:*** Make it a habit to visit your target neighborhood looking for possible deals. For Sale by Owner signs can be quite promising, but you can also look for homes that have been vacant for a long time, appear to be in need of repair, or even have for rent signs posted.

- ***Wholesalers:*** Let real estate wholesalers find the deals for you. Contact a few of them and get their list of possible properties.

If you have a little extra money to spend:

- **Start a Direct Mail Campaign:** Create your own letters or postcards to send to property owners in your target market. You can find the names and addresses by

Financial Freedom Investing

paying a list company. Some of these lists can be very lucrative:

- Absentee owner properties
- Multi-unit property owners
- Owner-occupied homes
- Recent evictions
- Delinquent property taxes
- Expired real estate listings
- Pre-foreclosure and foreclosure properties
- Estate and probate sales

- **Use your online presence:** Utilize social media. Set up a dedicated page to your real estate marketing plans on sites like Facebook, LinkedIn, Twitter, etc. Create an online business card to let people know what you're looking for.

- **Car/Yard Signs:** Invest in magnetic or vinyl signs for your car or yard.

- **Advertising:** Online or print advertising can get to areas that are difficult for you to reach on your own. Use resources like Google Adwords and don't neglect marketing in local newspapers, magazines, and radio. These efforts are a little pricey, but with the right strategy, they can get you good results fast.

6. **Make a Schedule**

You will need to set aside time to dedicate to your real estate venture. Be realistic with how much time you have to spend. Set your priorities first and then commit to the schedule you've set.

10 Important Features of Profitable Real Estate

To ensure that the property you choose is going to be profitable, it must have certain features. Even if it is a wreck and appears to be ready for demolition, there are still certain things you need to be sure of before your investment will be worthwhile. Here are the 10 most important features any property should have.

A Good Neighborhood

A look at the neighborhood can tell you a lot about the type of tenants you will attract. A location near a university will attract a lot of students. A location outside of the urban area may attract more families with children.

Property Taxes

All properties have taxes that need to be paid. You need to know how much they are and if the owners owe any back taxes. You can find out everything you need to know about the taxes with a visit to the county or city assessment office.

School System

If you are going to rent to families, you'll need to know something about the schools in the community. Few families are willing to buy or rent a home in a community with substandard schools.

Crime

Check with the local police department or visit the local library to see the latest crime statistics for the neighborhood. Pay extra attention to figures related to petty crimes, vandalism, and serious offenders.

Job Opportunities

Your best bet is to find properties in communities that are expanding their job market. These are more likely to attract buyers and renters to the area. Find out about job availabilities with the US Bureau of Labor Statistics. It can be a huge plus if major corporations are moving to the area. This kind of news often results in property values increasing as more people will be needed to fill those new jobs.

Neighborhood Amenities

What does the neighborhood have to offer? For children, there should be parks, playgrounds, movie theaters, etc. For adults, there should be fitness centers, public transportation, restaurants, and other entertainment venues.

Prospects for the Future

The city planning department should have information on any new developments that are proposed for the area. A lot of construction is a pretty good sign that the future is promising. However, be on the lookout for how those developments would impact property values.

Vacancies

When there are a lot of houses for rent or an excessive number of properties listed for sale, it could be a sign that the area is in a decline. Often when neighborhoods go into decline, property owners are forced to lower rents to keep their units occupied. On the other hand, when there are only a few vacancies in the area, you can comfortably ask for more rent.

Average Rent

If you're planning on renting, then you need to know just how much you can expect to get for a property in the area. You want to make sure that the rent will be enough to cover mortgage payments, property taxes, maintenance, and other forms of upkeep. Project these numbers into the future because what may be affordable today, could be marked out of your reach in five years, which may leave you forced to sell in an unfavorable market or go into bankruptcy later.

Exposure to Natural Disasters

It's not something that most people want to think about, but exposure to natural disasters can negatively impact your potential returns. Whether your home is in a flood zone, hurricane region, or earthquake-prone area, it's going to cost you either in insurance claims or direct repairs.

The best place to get reliable information is through government agencies, but don't stop there. The people in the community usually know everything about what's happening in the neighborhood. Talk to renters and property owners alike. Renters are more likely to give you a better picture since they have nothing to lose. They will tell you about any negatives you may not have thought of, but property owners will have a completely different perspective. If you keep these features in mind and your expectations realistic, you'll know when you've found the right property.

Top 15 Real Estate Investing Strategies

The strategies listed below are meant to give you an idea of the various ways you can generate your own income.

- **Flipping Houses:** Finding properties that need improvement, upgrading, or renovating and then reselling them at a profit.

- **Wholesaling:** Finding good deals on properties and then reselling them to a third party for an additional fee.

- **House Hacking:** Buy a multi-unit property and rent out the additional units. For example, buying a house and renting out the basement, or buying a duplex and renting out the extra unit.

- **BRRRR Investing:** Buy-Remodel-Rent-Refinance-Repeat. Buy a fixer-upper below market value, finance the property and then renovate. Refinance with a long-term mortgage and then take out your initial capital for a new investment.

- **The Cash Rental Strategy:** Buying property in cash. When you have completed the renovations and rented it out, you keep the majority of the money collected for yourself and can quickly invest in another property.

- **The Trade-Up Plan:** Using the IRS 1031 tax-free exchange to progressively trade up to bigger and better properties.

- **Hard Money Lending:** Giving short-term loans to investors who plan to fix-and-flip properties. Loans like these are usually given with high interest rates and up-front fees, so you'll make a good amount of cash in a short time.

- **Discounted Note Investing:** Buying real estate debt at a discount.

- **Syndications & Crowdfunding:** Pooling your money with individual investors to buy the perfect piece of property.

- **REITs:** Investing in companies that manage real estate. REIT stands for real estate investment trusts. You can buy REITs on the stock market, allowing you to own a small part of commercial real estate businesses and earn dividends on the profits in the interim.

Real estate can be a pretty lucrative business, but you have to be smart about it. There are many ways to achieve financial freedom through real estate, and each one has its own pros and cons. You can pick a strategy that works best for you or do several at a time. If one doesn't work right for you, then try another until you hit on your perfect match.

Chapter 7: Other Ways to Grow Wealth

The path to financial freedom can take you in many directions. Investing in the stock market and real estate are the most well-known entry points for new investors. They offer the lowest amount of risk in the investment world and give you a much better chance of success in the global marketplace.

That said, once you've gotten your feet wet and have acquired a taste for collecting passive money, you may want to start investing in other instruments that could prove to be even more lucrative for the private investor.

How to Start Investing in Exchange-Traded Funds (ETFs)

You've probably heard the term ETF mentioned in financial reports on the news and may not be sure of what it really is. You know it has something to do with the stock market, but you're not exactly sure about what they do.

ETFs or Exchange Traded Funds are groups of various investments that have been collected together to form one unit. These funds can be purchased on an exchange just like stocks with similar price movements.

Inside an ETF, you will find many different assets as opposed to a stock that will only be representative of only one asset. Because one share in an ETF covers so many assets, they are one of the easiest ways to diversify your portfolio. One ETF could possibly hold thousands of different stocks spread across several different industries.

Depending on the industries you may be interested in, you can purchase different types of ETFs.

- Bond ETFs consist of government, corporate, state, and municipal bonds.
- Industry ETFs can be compiled from stocks in a specific industry like banking, agriculture, or technology.
- Commodity ETFs would be a collection of different commodities like gold or oil.
- Currency ETFs include a selection of foreign currencies
- Inverse ETFs use the strategy of shorting various stocks. Shorting is the strategy of selling at a higher price and then repurchasing them after the price drops.

The only one on the list, the inverse ETFs are technically not exchange traded funds, but are actually exchange-traded notes or ETNs. These are bonds that are traded on the market like a stock and are banked by a bank.

Buying and selling ETFs

You can purchase ETFs through a broker. You have your choice of using either a traditional broker-dealer or an online broker. You can also use a robo-advisor, an automated investment system that uses certain algorithms to help you to build up your portfolio.

Advantages of ETFs

Financial Freedom Investing

As an investor, you can buy or sell a wide range of these securities with one single transaction. This also saves you on commission fees as well. You might even find some brokers who offer no-commission trading on ETFs, cutting your costs even more.

Aside from saving on commissions, there are other ways ETFs can save you money. They cost very little to operate and manage. Because they are tracking an index, it is more passively-managed requiring far less time to govern, and since they are widely diversified, their level of risk is much lower.

Disadvantages of ETFs

There are some ETFs that have higher fees. These are the ones that are generally focused on one single industry, so your diversification is extremely limited. There are also some ETFs that are actively managed by portfolio managers that do all of the buying and selling. These come with higher fees in order to pay the manager's fees for overseeing the fund's movements.

Indexed-Stocks ETFs

These funds provide investors the option to sell short, buy on margin, and acquire as little as one single share. If you choose to invest in Indexed-Stock ETFs, be watchful of those that might be heavily concentrated on one single industry or a limited number of stocks.

Dividends: Most ETFs pay dividends in proportion to their investment. As a result, you can expect to receive periodic payments for the earnings from the different securities for as long as you hold the fund. If for some reason, the fund is liquidated, you will receive your portion of its residual value.

Taxes

You'll also get to save, as these instruments are more tax-efficient that mutual funds. Because all trading happens through an exchange, there is no need to physically redeem the shares every time a transaction is completed. Since redeeming shares can trigger tax liabilities, conducting all transactions on the exchange keeps you from getting hit with taxes every time a transaction occurs.

Market Impact

Because of the increasing popularity of ETFs, more funds are now being created. This may not be good news for some investors since it means lower trading volumes for many of them. As more funds enter the market, it may become more difficult to buy and sell at such low volumes, which could leave you trapped in an instrument with no way out.

If you choose to invest in ETFs, make sure you select one that can help you to achieve your goals. You should feel confident that the fund you choose will give you the kind of exposure you need to grow your profits. Make sure that you're making your decision based on what works for you and not what others expect.

Start Making Money Now with Peer-to-Peer Lending

Another way to grow your wealth and gain financial freedom is with peer-to-peer lending. In the past, the only way to get a loan for a major purchase was through a financial institution. Now, you can become your own lending institution and collect interest on the money you loan to others. The majority of peer-to-peer loans are used for personal reasons like consolidating debt or home improvements.

Financial Freedom Investing

How it works

Making a loan with peer-to-peer lending is very different from how they are made with financial institutions. With a traditional loan, the bank will finance the loan with funds deposited from other customers. In contrast, peer-to-peer lending involves matching borrowers and investors through an online lending platform. As an investor, you decide which loans you want to issue and are free to reject those that don't interest you.

There are several lending platforms you can work with. Some have restrictions on the types of people that they allow to make loans, but there are some like the LendingClub.com and Prosper.com that are open to anyone who wants to participate as long as they meet the minimum deposit requirements.

Revenue is generated by charging interest and fees to the borrowers. Some fees including origination fees, late payment fees, and others can come to as much as 6% of the loan. The fee and interest charges vary depending on the platform you use, but be prepared to see some of that money evaporate when payments come in. The lending platform will take a percentage off of every payment made for themselves before sending the balance on to you.

Why peer-to-peer lending?

For the investor, you will receive a higher yield on your money than if you left it in a savings account. It is an easy alternative to investing than stocks and bonds. You don't need a lot of knowledge to get started. You are literally free to diversify your portfolio in any direction you want. And then there is the psychological advantage of knowing that you are doing something to contribute to the advancement of society in many different ways.

Disadvantages

Unlike with financial institutions, your money is not protected by the FDIC. So, if a borrower defaults on a loan, the chances of getting your investment back is slim to none. Also, you won't be able to cash in on your investment if you need the money back before the loan matures. The average term for a loan ranges between three to five years, leaving you without access to your funds for at least that amount of time.

Because this is such a new investment instrument, there is no track record or history to refer to. New trends are being set every day, so there's no way of telling whether or not the industry will continue to be stable.

It is possible to achieve huge returns (sometimes in the double-digits) with this type of lending, but don't allow those figures to distract you from reality. It is a risky investment tool, and you should always proceed with caution.

The 10 Best Strategies for Trading Cryptocurrencies

You've most likely been living under a rock if you haven't heard of cryptocurrencies yet. This new investment tool is believed by many to be the most promising means of garnering massive amounts of money extremely fast. Today, there are probably close to 2,000 altcoins to choose from, and the number is still growing.

Bitcoin, the first and by far the most profitable of cryptocurrencies has pushed itself into the world's consciousness with a whopping rise in price that escalated from a value worth pennies when it was first released to its highest point of nearly $20,000 in December of 2017. But with so many options to choose from, a new investor could easily be overwhelmed.

Financial Freedom Investing

While cryptocurrencies are probably the riskiest of all investment tools, it doesn't have to be that complicated. If you are brave enough to risk the highly volatile price movements and you think your heart can take the undulations of the waves, here are seven strategies that can help you get into this potentially lucrative market.

ICOs

ICOs or Initial Public Offerings can be very unpredictable because like the stock market's IPOs, these are new coins that are just getting started. When you purchase an ICO, you are literally getting in at the very beginning of a new coin. This means you're going to get the coin at a much lower price than it will be when it is released to the public. This automatically puts you in line for greater profits, sometimes as much as 2500% of your initial investment. However, because it is an entirely new coin, there is also a high risk that it will fail and take all of your money with it. Because there is no insurance protection for cryptocurrency investors, you need to do a lot of research to make sure that the team behind the coin are experienced enough to bring their new baby to life.

- Start by reviewing the list of new ICOs at https://icoranker.com/ and review the ones that interest you.

- Look for the purpose of the coin to determine its supply and demand. Coins that are designed for a limited population may not do well, but coins that have a potential to be useful for a large population can do much better.

- Once you've narrowed your list down to several viable choices, study the team members. You want to know their history, their background, their experience, and whether they can work together to meet the demands of the mission.

- Try to investigate a little further to find out what type of people are already investing in the coin. If they have a good community of investors who are optimistic about their future prospects, then you know they will support the coin and stick with it during the lean times. You can find this information by visiting the various forums set up for each coin.

- What is the legal framework between the development team and other contributors. You should find this information on the coin's whitepaper. The coin's terms and conditions should be laid out in a clear and easy to understand format.

- Visit the website and set-up an escrow wallet. You will be issued a private key you can use to sell your ICOs later.

If you decide to invest in ICOs, don't limit yourself to just one. It is easy for them to fail, so invest in several to increase your chances of success.

The best strategy for ICOs is the buy and hold strategy. The price will fluctuate wildly so don't go into a panic. Hold your coins until you see at least a 50% return on your investment before selling.

Low Price Accumulation

After a coin passes its ICO stage, it gets to join the big boys on the global marketplace. Just like with stocks, you want to buy the coins when the price is low and wait for it to go up in price. Most people will go into a panic when the price takes a significant drop, but seasoned cryptocurrency investors understand that extreme volatility is a characteristic of this type of investment.

Breakouts

By taking advantage of breakouts, you can cut down on your risks, but you need to recognize when these breakouts indicate the start of a new trend. The key to this strategy is to find the best time to enter the market by identifying areas of resistance or support that could be broken under the right conditions. In these scenarios, the coin could break through resistance upward or it can break through support and push downward.

Dollar Cost Averaging

Dollar cost averaging makes it possible for you to invest a pre-set amount of funds on a regular basis on each coin you want to buy. As a result, rather than finding the lowest or the highest price is no longer important. In essence, you are averaging out the overall cost of your coins with each payment. If done over a period of months, the prices generally come out much more favorably than if you were to make a single large payment.

Balanced

One key element in any type of investing is diversification. To successfully diversify, you need to balance your portfolio. This means investing in several different cryptos at the same time. When one coin goes into a slump you can still be earning profits on other coins.

Unbalanced

With an unbalanced strategy, investors designate a set percentage of their funds to coins based on their gut feeling about how well they expect it to perform in the future. Coins that are expected to do well are given the highest percentages while those that are not expected to perform as well will receive a lower percentage.

Profits Earned Reinvested in Other Coins

Once you've made a little money off of some cryptocurrencies, you can begin to diversify your portfolio even further by siphoning off some of your profits and investing them in new coins. By taking 50% of your earnings off of one coin and investing it in more successful coins, you can compound your success.

7 Must-Have Apps for Modern-Day Investors

Getting started in any type of investing can be tricky; even moreso for the new investor. One way to make things easier is to have a little help as you navigate all the potential pitfalls you'll face as you learn.

In the past, this kind of help was once only available to the privileged. Now, anyone can have the information available to capitalize on their growth. With the right apps to guide you, anyone can make decisions like a professional trader. Below are seven of the most effective apps all investors need to have at their disposal.

Financial Freedom Investing

Stash

The Stash mobile app is the go-to app for investors who are looking to access the best tools for the financial market. It makes it possible for you to purchase low-cost ETFs and stocks directly from your mobile device.

The cost is only $1/month, but for that low price, you get your own investment account and are allowed to make unlimited trades, free education, and the ability to make fractional purchases of more expensive stocks with payments as low as $5.

Vault

The Vault app focuses on older investors ready for retirement. It makes it possible for them to start an individual retirement account (IRA), Roth IRA, or a SEP IRA for those who are self-employed. Investors can direct a pre-set portion of their income automatically towards the plan they choose. So, even if you don't have a retirement plan with your company, you can start investing for a low monthly fee of $1.

Personal Capital

This app gives you regular updates and keeps track of all of the investments in your portfolio. It gives you a regular evaluation of how your investments are performing and suggestions on risk management. It is even possible to quickly check for which stocks are doing the best in your portfolio and which ones you need to make adjustments to. Personal Capital also gives you a comparison of how your portfolio performance measures up against the major market indices.

Stockpile

Stockpile allows you to invest in the stock market in smaller increments. You can buy fractional shares from hundreds of different stocks for as little as $5. There is a small commission fee of $0.99/trade, which is nominal when compared to other services that can charge as much as $10.00.

Parents or other adults can start their children off with a gift card for as little as $20. The small amount pays off in the long run as it starts the young ones off on the right foot learning money management early on.

Wealthfront

This app makes it easy to set aside cash for a college education. Users get a detailed look at their financial situation and can make investments designed to help them to appreciate their capital. You can start small and build as you go. Advice will be given based on the amount of risk you want to take and your financial goals.

E-Trade

E-Trade may seem a bit more expensive than some of the other apps, but with good reason. The app is designed so that researching and trading stocks is about as easy as it gets. You can trade stocks, ETFs, and mutual funds and get all your necessary data in real time. You can even get help in the best ways to build up your portfolio from one of their real live investment specialists.

Robinhood

Financial Freedom Investing

The Robinhood app opens the doors to new investors by allowing them to make small trades, all commission-free. This is the perfect app if you are still a little hesitant about getting into investing. You can buy stocks, options, ETFs, and cryptocurrencies all zero fees. Their new feature, Robinhood Gold, allows you to trade after-hours and gives you a line of credit so you can make larger purchases if you qualify. There isn't much in terms of trading, research, or personal support, but the platform is simple enough to use and who can beat a no-fee service.

The world of financial investments is changing. We live in a fast-moving digital age, and with more apps like these becoming available, it is now easier than ever for new investors to step on the stage and trade just like a pro.

Conclusion

No doubt, you have discovered a lot of information here that will stir up dreams and ideas for change. Together, we've learned how to break those financial chains so you can literally find your chance at freedom.

Think about it. It doesn't matter where you start, it only matters where you finish. Even if you're so deep in debt that you can't see your way out, it is possible to navigate that maze and find your way to freedom.

It all starts with changing your mind. When you can break those mental chains that may keep you in a "safety zone" then you are free to explore profitable opportunities around every corner. Actions, positive or negative, are the result of how we view our world. If you want to change your circumstances, start by changing your mind.

After identifying the right mindset, we learned how to change your present circumstances so you can get on a better financial footing. We discovered that budgeting can be exciting and enjoyable. Instead of being just an obligation, it becomes a tool for gaining control over your money.

From there, we moved on to how to better manage your credit. After all, if you're going to be growing wealth, good credit will be an essential part of it. This is the magic recipe that could change your life and guide you in the right direction.

But, we also discussed how being financially free meant more than just getting out of debt. We can choose to continue to work for our money or we could find ways to get our money to work for us. Knowing how to invest in stocks, bonds, real estate, or other lucrative opportunities can move us to take risks that we may never have thought about before.

Imagine how your life can change if you didn't have to work for every penny you made. Instead, money just enters your life effortlessly. How awesome would that be? Your health would be better, your mental state would improve, you'd anxiety will be replaced with joy and excitement. You'd be free to spend time with your family, take vacations together, or finally turn dreams into reality.

Whether you choose to invest in the stock market or cryptocurrency, whether you want to try your hand at bonds or real estate, you now have the keys to do whatever it is that you have always wanted to do. It'll take discipline and drive, but gaining that freedom can be one of the most liberating things in your life.

You now have a map to get you to your ultimate goal of financial freedom. Use this book as your guide and refer to it often, but don't just stop there. No matter how exciting and interesting you find the advice in these pages, there is only one way they will work to benefit you, and that's to put them into practice.

Some people can get overwhelmed with this much information and try to put off taking the first step until they understand better. That could delay your chances at success indefinitely. You don't need to know every detail about the stock market to start investing. You don't need to have all the fine points down to buy real estate. All you need is the heart and the desire to make it happen.

So, go ahead — stick your toe in the water and get started. It doesn't matter if you start small, as long as you take that first step. You have the keys to your own financial freedom here. Go back through these pages, create your plan, and get going. You're already halfway there; all that's left for you to do is go for it. There is no time like the present to change your life!